Twayne's United States Authors Series

EDITOR OF THIS VOLUME

Sylvia E. Bowman

Indiana University

Herman Melville

Revised Edition

TUSAS 37

Herman Melville

HERMAN MELVILLE

By TYRUS HILLWAY

REVISED EDITION

TWAYNE PUBLISHERS
A DIVISION OF G. K. HALL & CO., BOSTON

Published in 1979 by Twayne Publishers,
A Division of G. K. Hall & Co.
All Rights Reserved

Printed on permanent/durable acid-free paper and bound
in the United States of America

Library of Congress Cataloging in Publication Data

Hillway, Tyrus.
Herman Melville.

(Twayne's United States authors series ; TUSAS 37)
Bibliography: p. 163-71
Includes index.
1.   Melville, Herman, 1819-1891. 2.   Authors,
American—19th century—Biography.
PS2386.H5   1979   813'.3 [B]   78-11937
ISBN 0-8057-7256-1
0-8057-7433-5 (pbk.)

To Hazel
Who Loves Greylock

Contents

About the Author

Preface

Chronology

1. Young America in Literature   17
2. In Search of a Career   29
3. The White Whale Breaches   44
4. Return to Native Grounds   60
5. Loomings   68
6. The Everlasting No   78
7. Long Decline   113
8. Final Flowering   135
9. Epilogue: The Melville Revival   145
   Notes and References   154
   Selected Bibliography   163
   Index   172

About the Author

Long recognized as a leading authority on the life and works of Melville, Tyrus Hillway has devoted nearly forty years to Melville studies. He founded the Melville Society in 1945. He has recently returned to the United States after serving for several years as director of the American Studies program at the University of Salzburg (Austria).

Professor Hillway has held positions as dean at Hillyer College (now the University of Hartford), professor of English at Bridgeport University, president of Mitchell College (Conn.), professor of higher education and assistant to the president at the University of Northern Colorado, and is now co-director of the National Project for Improving Academic Administration. Besides publishing numerous articles on Melville in scholarly magazines, he was co-editor of the *Moby-Dick Centennial Essays* and prepared a modernized version of *Mardi* for the Twayne United States Classics Series. He has also published extensively in the field of American education.

Preface

Herman Melville was "rediscovered" by American readers of the 1920s after more than half a century of neglect. Interest in his writings has increased rapidly ever since, and studies of his life and works have appeared in great profusion. Since the first edition of the present book was issued in 1963, in fact, there have been more scholarly studies of Melville than of any other American author. This has necessitated the preparation of a revised edition to bring all material up to date and abreast of current research.

The book retains, however, its original purpose of providing an accurate and straightforward guide to an understanding of Melville and his works. It seeks to present only facts and reasonable interpretations rather than imaginative theories, no matter how exciting or persuasive. Because of his fondness for concealing metaphysical speculation and comment in symbolic form behind the incidents of his tales and novels, Melville has been subject more than most authors are to attempts by special-interest pleaders at fitting his ideas into a preconceived format of political, religious, or social belief. His writing is rich enough in literary symbolism and philosophical observation to open the way for exploitation by propagandists of many persuasions. "Correct" interpretations of *Moby-Dick* as an allegory, for example, have been abundant and mutually contradictory.

The Freudians had their fieldday with Melville in the twenties and thirties, when it was announced on the basis of Freudian theory that Melville, having been romantically involved with a native beauty of the South Seas, could never have been in love with his wife Lizzie, a cold Bostonian. The Marxists predictably seized upon Melville to support the socialist dogma, pretending to find in *Moby-Dick* and other works concealed attacks upon the American social and economic system. (With *Moby-Dick*, the Marxist argument came out in two opposite forms: in one, Captain Ahab was declared the symbolic representative of oppressive industrial institutions, the whaleship itself representing a factory; in another, it was not Ahab but the whale that stood for "capitalism," with Ahab serving as the tragic socialist hero fighting hopelessly against the evils of a free economy.) Critics with sectarian religious leanings either condemned Melville as an atheist or found him secretly sympathetic to their own beliefs. Homosexual critics, relying on a special insight, claimed Melville as one of their own. All such interpretations, of course, have stirred much interest in Melville's life and ideas but are equally unsupported by the factual evidence.

Except for strong objections to his antimissionary statements and some questioning of his veracity at the time his books first began to appear, the main critical turmoil over Melville has been the product of our own times. Nineteenth century readers admired his tales of romantic adventure but lost interest when his writing became too thoughtful. Twentieth century critics value Melville most for his brilliant probing of the human condition and seem to regard the narrative elements of his works chiefly as a welcome bonus.

In presenting materials about Melville's life and works, the present volume follows the same general plan of organization as that used in the earlier edition. Chapter 1 relates how Melville in his mid-twenties "accidentally" discovered his vocation as writer and how he learned and used the secrets of his craft. Chapters 2-4 deal with the principal facts of Melville's life and the events that surrounded the writing and publication of his books.

Chapters 5-8 examine Melville's works one by one, beginning with *Typee* (1846). Four novels of maritime adventure — *Typee, Omoo, Redburn* and *White-Jacket,* all partially autobiographical — are considered first. The three novels in which Melville revealed most of his deeper philosophical attitudes — *Mardi, Moby-Dick,* and *Pierre* — are then treated, following the example of Willard Thorp, as a kind of trilogy. The remaining works published within Melville's lifetime — *Israel Potter, The Piazza Tales, The Confidence-Man,* and the poetry — are discussed in one chapter. The final chapter in this group is devoted mainly to that jewel of Melville's old age, the posthumously published *Billy Budd.* Chapter 9 discusses briefly the Melville revival of the twentieth century.

The bibliography at the end of this book is highly selective. It includes only such works as are generally accessible to the serious-

Preface

minded reader seeking more detailed knowledge of Melville and his writings.

TYRUS HILLWAY

Salzburg, Austria

Chronology

1819 Herman Melville (or Melvill) born August 1 in New York City, third child of Allan and Maria Gansevoort Melvill.

1825– Attends New-York Male High School.
1830

1830 Allan Melvill's importing business fails, and family moves to Albany, New York. Herman enrolls at the Albany Academy from October 15, 1830, until his father's death.

1832 January 28, Allan Melvill dies, heavily in debt.

1832– Works as a bank clerk, as helper on his uncle's farm in Pitts-
1837 field, Massachusetts, and as assistant in his brother Gansevoort's fur factory and store. Enters Albany Classical School (1835).

1837 Teaches school near Pittsfield.

1838 May, the Melvilles move from Albany across the river to Lansingburgh, New York. Studies surveying at the Lansingburgh Academy.

1839 "Fragments from a Writing Desk" published May 14 and 18 in the *Democratic Press and Lansingburgh Advertiser.* June 5, ships as a crew member aboard the *St. Lawrence,* a packet boat plying between New York and Liverpool; October 1, he returns. Teaches school at Greenbush, New York.

1840 Works briefly as a substitute teacher in Brunswick, New York. Travels with Eli James Fly to visit his uncle Thomas in Galena, Illinois.

1841 January 3, ships as a common seaman aboard the whaling ship *Acushnet,* bound from Fairhaven, Massachusetts (New Bedford harbor), for the South Seas.

1842 July 9, deserts ship with Richard T. Greene at Nuku Hiva in the Marquesas Islands. After a month among supposedly cannibalistic natives of the Taipi valley, escapes on August 9 by joining the crew of the *Lucy Ann,* an Australian whaler. Placed ashore at Tahiti with other crewmen and held in light confinement as an accused mutineer.

1843   Spends May to August at Lahaina (Maui) and Honolulu. Works in Honolulu during the summer. August 17, enlists in the United States Navy at Honolulu as an ordinary seaman and sails for home.

1844   October 14, mustered out of the navy in Boston and returns to Lansingburgh. Begins writing the story of his adventures that winter.

1846   *Typee* published. "The Story of Toby" published and later added to the book as an epilogue.

1847   *Omoo.* August 4, marries Elizabeth Shaw. Efforts to secure a government appointment in Washington prove fruitless; settles in New York City.

1847–   Tries earning his living as a writer. Closely associated with
1850   Evert and George Duyckinck and other literary figures of New York. Writes reviews and articles for *The Literary World* and *Yankee Doodle* magazines.

1849   February 16, son Malcolm born. *Mardi* and *Redburn* published. October 11, sails for Europe to arrange publication of *White-Jacket.*

1850   *White-Jacket.* Takes his family to Pittsfield, Massachusetts, for the summer. September, purchases a farm (later named Arrowhead) at Pittsfield, settling there as a gentleman-farmer and author. Meets and forms strong friendship with Nathaniel Hawthorne, then living at nearby Lenox. Writes an enthusiastic review of Hawthorne's *Mosses from an Old Manse.*

1851   *Moby-Dick.* October 22, son Stanwix born.

1852   *Pierre.*

1853   May 22, daughter Elizabeth born. Unsuccessful in efforts to secure a consular appointment. December 10, copies of his books destroyed in the disastrous Harper and Brothers fire.

1853–   Writes stories and sketches for *Putnam's Monthly Magazine*
1856   and *Harper's New Monthly Magazine.*

1855   *Israel Potter* published in book form after serialization in *Putnam's*. March 2, daughter Frances born.

1856   *The Piazza Tales.* Travels abroad, partly for his health, leaving New York for Europe October 11.

1857   *The Confidence-Man.* May 5, sails from Liverpool for New York.

1857–   Earns money as a lecturer for three seasons. Topics: "Statu-

1860	ary in Rome," "The South Seas," "Traveling." Begins writing poetry about 1859.
1860	Sails for both health and pleasure aboard the clipper ship *Meteor,* commanded by his younger brother Thomas. Leaves ship at San Francisco, returning home by way of Panama.
1863	Moves from Pittsfield to New York City, exchanging homes with his younger brother Allan.
1865	A pirated edition of *Israel Potter* published in Philadelphia as *The Refugee.*
1866	*Battle-Pieces and Aspects of the War* published, some of the poems having appeared previously in *Harper's.* December 5, appointed a district inspector of customs for New York harbor.
1867	September 11, son Malcolm killed by his own gun under tragic circumstances.
1876	*Clarel.*
1885	December 31, resigns his position as inspector of customs.
1886	Son Stanwix dies in a San Francisco hospital.
1888	Makes a short vacation voyage to Bermuda. *John Marr and Other Sailors.*
1891	*Timoleon.* Melville dies September 28.
1924	*Billy Budd* published posthumously.

CHAPTER 1

Young America in Literature

I The Unfolding Within

EARLY in the year 1846 there appeared on the American literary scene — after prior publication in England because of the conditions of copyright then prevailing — a book by a young writer hitherto unknown which was destined shortly to start a new and exciting literary vogue, to launch an unemployed sailor on a briefly successful career as author, and to foreshadow the creation a few years later of one of the world's undoubted masterpieces. The book was *Typee,* a romance of adventure in the South Seas, produced by a brilliant and cultured but poverty-ridden young man from Lansingburgh, New York, whose name was Herman Melville. *Typee* made the immediate reputation, though not the fortune, of its author; and it attracted a host of delighted and only half-believing readers with a suspenseful account of Melville's dangerous and fascinating sojourn, during the course of a South Seas whaling cruise, among a tribe of reputed cannibals.

Melville was never to be what one would call today a "successful" author. Except for the brief moment of public recognition at the beginning of his career, his writings during his lifetime failed either to bring him a decent income to support his family or to arouse more than a fairly small following of readers. None of his works would have won a prize for literature in its day or appeared on what we now call the "best-seller list." While other professional authors of the mid-nineteenth century (especially women) were succeeding well in catering to the public taste, Melville's publishers, both at home and abroad, began to show reluctance quite early in the game to risk further investment in his productions. When he died in 1891, his works had been relegated, except by a few enthu-

17

siasts, to the dust heap of adolescent adventure stories, and he was well-nigh forgotten both as author and as man.

Literary fashions being what they are, many of today's most highly praised and best-selling novels will shortly vanish into the oblivion they richly deserve. Other works, appreciated now by a small circle of readers, will gradually achieve recognition as worthy contributions to literature. Something of this kind occurred in the case of Melville. In what was generally regarded as the most authoritative history of American literature published at the turn of the century, Barrett Wendell of Harvard gave him only a single, rather condescending sentence. Yet in the twentieth century Melville's fame has advanced so rapidly that he is now generally considered one of our three or four preeminent novelists. *Moby Dick*, his masterwork of metaphysics and the sea, is hailed by critics throughout the world as one of the great literary accomplishments of all time. But the story of the artist unappreciated by his own generation is hardly new in history. For additional American examples, we need only recall such important figures as Thoreau, Whitman, Henry James, and Emily Dickinson.

Though deeply interested in literature from boyhood, Melville became an author almost by accident. As a career, authorship for the son of a merchant and nephew of bankers could hardly be considered a practical choice. Scion of two famous American patriot families and heir to a tradition of gentility, he was to spend most of his adult life attempting to maintain and live up to the family tradition while at the same time seeking an acceptable way to make a living for himself and his growing family. Until he discovered his talent for telling a story at about the age of twenty-five and saw commercial possibilities in it, he must have looked upon literary composition as only a pleasant and gentlemanly avocation. Once launched in the field, however, he gave it all his energy and attention. He became not only a powerful writer of prose but — more and more as he continued to write his books — a deep speculator about the universe and the human condition.

Writing released in Melville the powers of a penetrating mind and a vivid imagination. "Until I was twenty-five," he said in a much-quoted letter to his friend and neighbor Nathaniel Hawthorne, "I had no development at all. From my twenty-fifth year I date my life. Three weeks have scarcely passed, at any time between then and now, that I have not unfolded within myself."[1] Thus in exulting tones — though he added in the same letter a mention of his odd fear that he had "now come [in his early thirties!] to the inmost leaf of the bulb, and that shortly the flower must fall to the mould" — Melville remarked upon his joyful chance discovery, not long after his return from the South Seas in 1844, of his vocation in literature. His decision to write and the mental growth it produced in him came unexpectedly and after a series of false starts. As a boy he had confidently considered commerce as his chosen career and as a young man had seen hopes for a future in surveying, schoolteaching, and the sea before turning seriously to writing. When he at length put words on paper to recount the narrative of his Pacific adventures, a delayed shock of recognition occurred; and, having had experiences of intense interest that could form a basis for his plots, he now recognized in authorship the career for which his talents were formed.

Willard Thorp, in what still remains an excellent introduction to the study of Melville's works,[2] has discerningly pointed out the fact that the author of *Moby-Dick* was not, contrary to the opinion of some nineteenth-century critics, a "natural genius" who composed novels effortlessly and with scant attention to technique. As he "unfolded within himself," Melville also became increasingly conscious of the role of style in literary narration. Investigations of his methods of composition confirm Thorp's view of him as a writer thoroughly aware of the technical aspects of his art, as one who carefully analyzed his own creative powers and related them to the spiritual problems with which he struggled philosophically.

In such works as *Mardi, Pierre,* and *The Confidence-Man,* as well as others, Melville's preoccupation with questions of literary craftsmanship is clearly and frankly shown. He confessed with a tinge of puzzled vexation in *Mardi,* his earliest attempt at ambitious writing, to having produced a large part of the book in haphazard fashion and without a fixed plan to guide him. The compelling current of the work, he complained, swept him irresistibly along on a chartless course, exerting so much domination over his imagination as to make holding the literary tiller with a firm hand well-nigh impossible. *Mardi* is a brilliant work in many ways, but it lacks form and unity of effect. The fact that Melville understood this, however vaguely, and expressed concern over his loss of control of his materials only emphasizes the more his growing interest in the techniques of his craft. Years afterward, in his poem on "Art" — the manuscript of which betrays by its numerous revisions and corrections much about its author's habits of composi-

tion — he stated with a degree of confidence based on long experience a writer's creed reflecting the attitude of a conscious artist
who aspires to literary perfection:

> In placid hours well-pleased we dream
> Of many a brave unbodied scheme.
> But form to lend, pulsed life create,
> What unlike things must meet and mate:
> A flame to melt — a wind to freeze;
> Sad patience — joyous energies;
> Humility — yet pride and-scorn;
> Instinct and study; love and hate;
> Audacity — reverence. These must mate
> And fuse with Jacob's mystic heart,
> To wrestle with the angel — Art.[3]

Such lines have the ring of truth, and they indicate Melville's
lifelong concern for literary effect as well as his willingness to
perspire in the cause of literature.

II   *Symbolism in Melville*

The style of Melville's best prose has been described as rich,
turgid, allusive, and highly imaginative — even as poetic. Readers
of his poetry are frequently amazed at the relative conciseness and
unlyrical barrenness of the verse in contrast with his prose. Parts of
his finest novels and shorter tales appear so crammed with descrip-
tive detail, dramatic tension, references to his reading, and suggestive symbolism as to be well-nigh overwhelming. The literary diet in
a *Mardi* or a *Moby-Dick* is emotionally rich and intellectually
complex; by contrast, such a straightforward narrative as *Typee*
begins to strike one as thin and spare in style. From *Typee* to *Moby-
Dick* the reader of Melville can trace in the writing a rapid and
fairly steady development from the lucid, fast-moving, realistic
storytelling methods of a nineteenth-century Swift or Defoe to a
more colorful, beautifully rhythmic, sometimes rhapsodic style e-
laborate in its music and symbols.

Much — perhaps far too much — has been said about Melville's
use of symbolism. The major portion of *Mardi* extends even
beyond symbolism into allegory, and several of the other works —
White-Jacket, Moby-Dick, The Confidence-Man, and *Billy Budd*
— may be seen to have something of an allegorical framework.
Particular attention has been paid by scholars and by various ama-

teurs to suspected hidden meanings in *Moby-Dick,* and a number
of ingenious and highly plausible "interpretations" have been proposed.[4] For those who are willing to take him at his word, Melville
provided a satisfactory explanation of his intentions in his remarks
to Sophia Hawthorne when the book first appeared. His words, in
reply to her apparent inquiry about an allegorical interpretation,
were: "I had some vague idea while writing it, that the whole book
was susceptible of an allegorical construction, & also that *parts* of it
were — but the speciality of many of the particular subordinate al-
legories, were first revealed to me, after reading Mr Hawthorne's
letter, which, without citing any particular examples, yet intimated
the part-&-parcel allegoricalness of the whole."[5]

Scholars of the past stubbornly disbelieved or blandly ignored
this clear-cut and seemingly unequivocal statement by the man who
should have known most about the symbolism used in *Moby-Dick.*
Although it may be argued that Melville had reasons for concealing
his allegorical intentions after the hullabaloo aroused by *Mardi* and
although, granted certain premises, one can find in the work various overall interpretations that hang together very well, no sup-
portable reason exists to affirm that Melville deliberately lied about
the matter. Close examination of his major plots tends to indicate
that he was telling the truth quite simply and frankly. Most of his
books may be "susceptible of an allegorical construction"; yet,
after *Mardi,* his concern can be seen to have been in symbolism for
enrichment of details and incidents rather than for "the part-&-
parcel allegoricalness of the whole."

The tendency toward symbolical description and incident in
Melville obviously resembles that in Hawthorne. It is this resemblance and their interest in similar themes,[6] more than mere physical propinquity and concurrence in time, that justify one in placing
Hawthorne and Melville in the same category of American literature. The ability to see in ordinary objects and events more than
pure objective reality, to sense moral, spiritual, and aesthetic values
and parallels, and thus to vitalize their works with philosophically
suggestive connotations is the quality that principally accounts for
the vast power of both men as writers. All Melville's books after
Omoo reveal his increasing delight in looking beyond the fact, in
relating the trivial detail to a massive spiritual generalization.
Sometimes this habit results in a mere figure of speech, as when in
White-Jacket an official summons to the crew of the *Neversink* to

witness a flogging is rendered ominous by comparing it indirectly to the fateful call of the archangel Gabriel's final trumpet.[7] Sometimes the result is a passage more explicit and more detailed, as when in *Moby-Dick* the author exhaustively reflects upon the mystical effects of whiteness[8] or when he shows Captain Ahab discussing with Starbuck his deeper and more personal reasons for pursuing the white whale:

All visible objects, man, are but as pasteboard masks. But in each event — in the living act, the undoubted deed — there, some unknown but still reasoning thing puts forth the mouldings of its features from behind the unreasoning mask. If man will strike, strike through the mask! How can the prisoner reach outside except by thrusting through the wall? To me, the white whale is that wall, shoved near to me. Sometimes I think there's naught beyond. But 'tis enough. He tasks me; he heaps me; I see in him outrageous strength, with an inscrutable malice sinewing it. That inscrutable thing is chiefly what I hate; and be the white whale agent, or be the white whale prinicpal, I will wreak that hate upon him.[9]

The prevalence of such examples of symbolism in Melville's works has tempted some readers to seek allegorical meanings even in *Typee* or to build out of Melville's love of symbols a wholly new symbolism of their own. This temptation is one that new readers of Melville would be wise to avoid.

III *Use of Sources*

Of particular importance in the development of Melville's literary style was his unusual competence as an assimilator of materials from numerous different sources. These materials came primarily from his own experience and from his reading. Unlike Poe or Henry James, Melville exhibited little brilliance in the invention of plots. He derived his ideas frequently from incidents in his own life — a habit that for a time caused his biographers to regard nearly everything he wrote as autobiography. He also drew freely upon source books, either those he searched out for a particular purpose or those he happened simply to be reading for his own enjoyment. Though his imagination created some of his plots, especially for the shorter pieces, his forte did not lie so much in literary invention as in philosophical, dramatic, and artistic elaboration. This trait may partly account for the dwindling of his literary output after the 1850s; he had used up the stock of sources upon which he drew for his plots and characters.[10] He made literary grist of almost everything noteworthy in his past experience, combining with it voluminous matter from other authors. Admittedly he was a great borrower. He dipped shamelessly into source book after source book, sometimes acknowledging his debt but more often skillfully transmuting the contraband from its original state into something different and quite his own.

His actual borrowing has been traced with considerable accuracy by scholars like Charles R. Anderson, for *Typee* and *Omoo*;[11] Howard P. Vincent, for *Moby-Dick*;[12] and a host of others. The significance of the question involves not so much the nature and extent of his borrowing but the use he made of it. Thorp has commented on the manner in which Melville, while writing *Typee*, employed materials from C. S. Stewart's *A Visit to the South Seas in the U. S. Ship Vincennes*.[13] Apparently Melville, to refresh his memory and also to authenticate his own statements regarding the South Seas region and its islanders, kept Stewart's book open on the desk beside him while he wrote.[14] As Thorp makes clear, Stewart's work is a sober treatise describing what its author saw and offering various explanations or generalizations based on a careful weighing of the observable evidence. Melville's book, on the contrary, is a delightful story in which the anthropological and geographical facts are subtly subordinated to the dramatic requirements of the yarn itself. Stewart's main points and ponderous conclusions are presented by Melville as personal impression or hearsay.

Since Melville read so voraciously and borrowed so copiously, the burrowings of scholars will continue to unearth examples of his literary larceny for a good while to come. As an example of its importance to his writing, one may recall that, by actual page count, nearly a quarter of *Moby-Dick* is known to consist of cetological and whaling information taken from Thomas Beale's *The Natural History of the Sperm Whale* and a handful of other scientific sources.[15] Yet Melville's powers of assimilation and of transmutation were so skillful, even when he came close to quoting source material almost verbatim, that the improvements in the final product over the original seem as mountainous as the White Whale himself. In *Moby-Dick*, as in most of Melville's best work, the reader discovers a remarkable blending of the author's recollected experience, his voluminous reading, and the leaven of metaphorical philosophizing. Melville's least admirable works are those in which these elements have been unevenly blended — in which, for example, the philosophical comments appear digressive. His best works are those in which personal experience and observation, source materials, and philosophical comment are blended through symbolism into an artistic unity.

IV *Melville's Humor*

In one of the most interesting but least perceptive criticisms of American literature ever concocted, the British writer D. H. Lawrence, who seems to have had absolutely no sense of humor, labeled Melville a man who "hated the world" and whose chief literary importance lay in his predicting the "Doom! Doom! Doom!" of white America. While praising some parts of *Moby-Dick* and recognizing elements of greatness in it, Lawrence deplored what he termed sententiousness and sermonizing in the work. He accused Melville of having a poor style and of being misled by Emersonian morality.[16] Thoroughly anti-American, Lawrence was hardly the person to recognize and appreciate the rich humor (sometimes bawdy) in *Moby-Dick* or the brilliant, satirical wit in such tales as *Mardi*.

American critics have themselves occasionally suffered from a similar lapse of judgment. One popular introduction to a modern edition of *Moby-Dick* even refers to Melville as a "kind of Gloomy Gus" — thus ignoring the comic manner in which much of the story is presented. In almost every one of Melville's novels from *Typee* to the first part of *Pierre* not the least attractive quality of the style is a bubbling mirth and wit. The humor of such early works as *Typee* and *Omoo* is generally broad, good-natured, and easily appreciated. In *Mardi* the comic elements consist more often in witty philosophical sallies or social and political satire. *Moby-Dick* is replete with a type of humor strongly reminiscent of Rabelais and Shakespeare; special emphasis is placed on the comedy of sex.

Rosenberry reminds one of a fact seldom noticed by other critics — that Melville made his reputation in the nineteenth century largely as a humorist.[7] In the very first chapter of *Typee* one finds Melville expressing his amusement at the slightly shocking account of a South Seas lady who embarrased the officers and men of a French warship by impulsively displaying for their edification the tattooing on intimate portions of her body. Not only *Typee* but *Omoo, Redburn, White-Jacket,* and the major part of *Mardi* can be seen to have been written in a lighthearted vein which to a considerable extent accounts for their charm. They abound in jokes and comic episodes relating to gastronomy, self-ridicule, gentle sarcasm, irony, intentional exaggeration of detail, and pure playfulness. *Moby-Dick* suggests by its humor a book written principally for men. The phallic symbolism of such a chapter as "The Cassock" probably had little meaning or interest for the ladies of Melville's generation, though most male readers find it humorous. More generally appreciated is the chapter on "Fast-Fish and Loose-Fish," in which Melville, to illustrate a point of law, wittily cites a British court case involving adultery. In it

a gentleman, after in vain trying to bridle his wife's viciousness, had at last abandoned her upon the seas of life; but in the course of years, repenting of that step, he instituted an action to recover possession of her. Erskine [counsel for the defendant] was on the other side; and he then supported it by saying, that though the gentleman had originally harpooned the lady, and had once had her fast, and only by reason of the great stress of her plunging viciousness, had at last abandoned her; yet abandon her he did, so that she became a loose-fish; and therefore when a subsequent gentleman re-harpooned her, the lady then became that subsequent gentleman's property, along with whatever harpoon might have been found sticking in her. (chap. 89)

After *Pierre* a more serious vein, with greater stress on irony, can be detected in Melville's writing. Possibly the change came about as the result of the public's failure to understand Melville and the consequent frustration he felt. In *The Confidence-Man,* which was probably intended by Melville to be a humorous book, there is an underlying note of bitterness. It contains more irony and less fun. "Benito Cereno," too, lacks the sprightly, playful touches of Melville's earlier stories. Nevertheless, among the works written after *Pierre* (1852), there occur such charmingly semicomic pieces as "The Piazza" and "I and My Chimney" — both, in spite of serious undertones, excellent examples of the kind of sentimental humor that Melville did best. Several of the tales offer startling examples of Melville's penchant for mixing humor with biting social criticism. "The Tartarus of Maids" conceals very specific sexual symbolism in a description of the plight of women factory workers,[18] and "I and My Chimney" has been interpreted by Sealts as a symbolical defense by Melville of his claim to sanity.[19]

V *Religion and Science*

Nineteenth-century America was Platonic in its philosophy and mainly traditional in its religious ideas. Though sects of many differing kinds flourished, the basic authority of the Bible was regarded with great reverence, and skeptics were treated with suspicion. At the same time, naturalistic science was emerging rapidly as an increasingly influential factor in modern civilization, and its discoveries generally denied the truth of much religious teaching. The conflict produced a great deal of distress in the minds of conscientious thinkers. The mental anguish of the nineteenth century is rarely to be found among educated Americans today, when science has clearly become the major influence in our lives. But the triumph of science did not occur until the later part of the last century. Symbolic of the victory was the publication of Darwin's *Origin of Species* in 1859. Even Emerson, the Platonic leader of the Romantic Age in America, had the shrewdness to recognize and comment upon the profound changes produced by scientific advance in all aspects of our life.

Melville's broad interests and intellectual independence, along with the special nature of his experiences, placed him far ahead of his literary contemporaries in the appreciation of science. In a period when college-educated writers like Hawthorne still thought of science as a kind of dangerous magic and when the schools were teaching science mainly to impress children with heaven's power and beneficence, Melville's distrust of romantic optimism and his reluctant acceptance of a scientific view of nature shocked and repelled his readers. More important for his art, the same struggle between authoritarian religion and modern science that was being waged in the intellectual world of the day (see Andrew Dickson White, *A History of the Warfare of Science with Theology in Christendom*) was fought furiously in Melville's mind and heart, and the battle smoke and wounds appear throughout his works from *Mardi* on.

Though romantic in his literary antecedents as he was Calvinistic in his religious nurture, Melville possessed the intellectual integrity to see that neither the enthusiastic, nature-worshipping romanticism nor the stubbornly antiscience Christianity of his time could stand up successfully to scientific realism. By instinct and early training a romanticist but by self-conducted spiritual search a realist, Melville never quite reconciled these opposing points of view in his own mind or in his books. He devoted much of his literary effort (and lost his readers in the process) to attacking romantic excesses while making liberal use of romantic language and conventions. He openly scorned the popular concept of nature (instilled by Rousseau) as harmlessly beautiful and friendly to man, the thoughtless optimism, the oversentimentalism, and the other pleasant weaknesses of the Romantic Age. On the other hand, he saw in science, though objective and realistic, something cold and even threatening. If a choice were demanded between the head and the heart, between intellect and feeling, he stood (he said) for the heart. By the end of his lifetime industrial technology, literary realism, and an analytical attitude toward individuals not only were accepted but had become the fashion; during his creative years, however, they were only vaguely foreshadowed for most Americans, and for Melville they constituted new and beckoning but still uneasily unfamiliar ground.

The tempestuous excitements and bitterly fought stalemates that occurred in Melville's mind (leading neither to slow tragedy nor to "an utter wreck," as a few critics have suggested) resulted from his living, like Carlyle's Teufelsdröckh, between two intellectual worlds: "the one already dead, the other powerless to be born." In such a mental and spiritual environment, little wonder that for Melville, during the years of his greatest achievement, the intellectual and moral world appeared as consisting not merely in a duality of good and evil, truth and falsehood, but in endless and soul-defying ambiguities.

VI *The Eagle in the Soul*

While Melville was descended on the paternal side from aristocratic forebears, he was a strong believer in the American ideals of liberty and equality. His personal pride in his family background stemmed mainly from the part his two grandfathers had played in freeing the country from British rule and the British class system. Though he often pointed out in his writings ways in which American society fell short of achieving the ideals on which the Constitution was based, he staunchly supported democratic principles. His social criticism, to the extent that it is included within his writings, was directed not against the American system itself but against the evils within human nature.[20]

What makes Melville worthy of a place in the front ranks of the world's literary masters is not merely his unquestionable talent for creating word-pictures and his acute and perspicacious observation of life in its true details but, even more, his intense dedication to intellectual honesty. No American writer was ever more conscientiously honest in depicting the truth as he saw it. Such honesty, of course, does not make for popularity. While many best-selling authors are seen to achieve success through intellectual charlatanism, honesty of Melville's kind seems to require long consideration on the reader's part and a passage of time before eventual appreciation.

Melville's development as a writer followed no ordinary pattern. Discovering his literary abilities rather late in the game and almost accidentally, he flowered quickly — not as a "natural" artist who could spin yarns endlessly and without effort but as a struggling apprentice willing to toil for long, arduous hours to learn his craft. The very rapidity of his artistic development, however, together with his eagerness to experiment, resulted in certain faults or weaknesses in a number of his books — the faults, mainly, of artistic immaturity. Eager to please, he justifiably expected greater acclaim from his public as his techniques improved; but the reverse occurred. Unfortunately, Melville was never psychologically attuned to a precise knowledge of what the public wanted; therefore, he was writing at the end of his career almost exclusively to please himself. Nor could he content himself in his writing with being a mere entertainer. He launched himself recklessly on the dangerous quest for philosophical truth; and he held it his duty to reveal to others what he learned, harsh and unpalatable though it might be. The search and his many personal disappointments convinced him at last that the world can be a dark and vicious place; to find humor and brightness there in the face of this conviction required courage of the highest order. Such courage Melville possessed. His moral and spiritual strength in a world not entirely to his liking shines brightly through his works and may be seen also in the circumstances of his life.

CHAPTER 2

In Search of a Career

I "Son-of-a-Gentleman"

THE STORY of Herman Melville's years from young adolescence to mature manhood is largely the story of his confused and frantic search for a career. Born in the city of New York on August 1, 1819, Melville was the third child and second son of Allan Melvill,[1] a wholesale merchant and importer then living in comfortable economic circumstances, and of Maria Gansevoort Melvill, only daughter of "the richest man in Albany," the respected and wealthy General Peter Gansevoort, hero of the defense of Fort Stanwix during the American Revolution. On the paternal side, his ancestry, though not so prosperous as on the maternal, was equally distinguished. Old Major Thomas Melvill, his grandfather, had been one of the "Indians" who took part in the Boston Tea Party during the events leading to the war and had then served his country creditably throughout the hostilities.[2] On the mantlepiece of the Major's home in Boston there stood, all during Herman's boyhood, a bottle of the tea shaken from his grandfather's clothes after the Tea Party and collected as a memento of this glorious occasion.[3] All his life Herman retained the sense of his family's importance to American history and its links with European aristocracy; he was often rather shocked by the serene indifference of his fellow Americans to its claims upon their gratitude — or, at the very least, their remembrance.

Herman's boyhood could not have been other than an extremely happy one. He lived in a home in which all the members loved one another deeply. He enjoyed opportunities from his earliest childhood of observing cultured, even somewhat ceremonious, behavior in his parents; of hearing conversation in which political and

29

literary topics were freely discussed; and of becoming accustomed to the society of books. He attended from about the age of seven until 1830, the New-York Male High School, where he may have languished somewhat in the shadow of his brilliant older brother Gansevoort. Here he studied under the then-popular Lancastrian or monitorial system the usual curriculum of the day, including — as he indicated in a boyish letter to his grandmother — geography, grammar, arithmetic, writing, speaking, spelling, and a little science.[4] Although his parents pretended to regard him during his childhood as "very backward in speech and somewhat slow in comprehension," Herman soon gave signs of ability in public speaking and eventually won recognition by being selected one of the monitors in the school. Nevertheless, his father, convinced that his possibilities for intellectual attainment were limited, marked him for commerce rather than for a profession.[5]

As Allan Melville's business flourished and his family steadily grew, he occupied in turn larger and more fashionable houses. In 1828 he moved into a fine house with an ample garden and yard at 675 Broadway. By 1830 there were eight children in the Melville household. They included, besides Herman and his older brother Gansevoort (born 1815) and sister Helen Maria (1817), a troop of younger children: Augusta (1821), Allan (1823), Catherine (1825), Priscilla Frances (1827), and Thomas (1830). The pleasant, cultured, and socially active existence of the Melvilles was abruptly shattered, however, by alarming business reverses. His credit having been overextended, in spite of considerable financial assistance from his father the old Major, Allan in the spring of 1830 found himself helpless to lay hands upon ready cash necessary to meet a particular note. As a result, the entire credit structure of the firm collapsed; Allan, like many another businessman during those months of economic panic, was forced into bankruptcy. After futile attempts to reestablish himself, he eventually found it expedient to accept the management of a New York fur company's branch in Albany.

After moving to Albany in the autumn of 1830, Allan by strenuous work slowly regained his financial footing. He sent his three oldest boys to the Albany Academy, a highly respected private school. Herman, who no doubt was registered not for the traditional classical course of study but for the commercial course, won a copy of the elaborate literary annual, *The Carcanet*, for excellence in bookkeeping — a prize for which in later life he evinced little but embarrassment. His brother Gansevoort, meanwhile, was winning distinction in such classical subjects as ancient history, Roman antiquities, penmanship, English, and Latin composition.

Just as fortune seemed again to be favoring him and as his family's life settled back into familiar patterns, Allan Melville's business affairs once again suffered a setback. Excessive worry and overwork finally took their toll upon his health. By January, 1832, he was both physically and mentally very ill. His brother Thomas, notified in Pittsfield by the Gansevoorts that Allan might not recover, made the long, hilly journey across the Housatonic and Hudson river valleys from the Berkshire country of Massachusetts to find Allan in delirium. Thomas quickly made up his mind that the patient had lapsed into permanent insanity and for this reason actually hoped against his recovery. On January 28, 1832, Allan Melville died. The shock of his father's financial collapse and then his tragic death only slightly more than a year later under circumstances of considerable horror inflicted a wound upon Herman's mind and spirit that probably scarred him for the rest of his life. He was to draw upon this memory two decades later while writing *Pierre.*

After the loss of their father, the two older sons took charge of the family's pecuniary problems with resourcefulness and bravery. At seventeen, having learned something of business methods by substituting for his father in management of the fur company during the latter's final illness, Gansevoort was now launched through his mother's backing and that of Uncle Peter Gansevoort in a fur business of his own. The enterprise was rewarded with almost immediate success. Herman, though not yet thirteen, was placed in a position as apprentice clerk in an Albany bank where he worked quietly and apparently with little enthusiasm during the next two years. The Melvilles for a time achieved a measure of prosperity and lived once more in the style to which they had accustomed themselves in New York City. The girls of the family attended the rather fashionable Albany Female Academy.

Possibly because of his mother's concern over his health, Herman in the spring of 1834 left his position at the bank and spent a season working for his Uncle Thomas on the latter's farm near Pittsfield. In a history of that city to which he contributed a sketch in later life, Melville described his uncle as a kindly, mild-mannered gentleman with "a faded brocade of old French breeding."[6] Thomas, though now reduced unwillingly to farming, had once been a wealthy banker in Paris and had married the daughter of a prominent French banking family. Losing his fortune, he had made a retreat into western Massachusetts and had there been commissioned a major during the War of 1812. He had fourteen children, six by his first wife and eight by his second, but not all were still alive during Herman's first summer in Pittsfield. One of them, Pierre Thomas (commonly addressed as Cousin Tom), was away at sea and was noteworthy for having taken part in the famous cruise of the U.S.S. *Vincennes* to the Pacific Ocean. Tom was destined, unfortunately, to become a hopeless drunkard and eventually to lose his life while on a whaling cruise. Another cousin, Priscilla, may very well have suggested to Melville the strange character Isabel in his novel *Pierre*. Like Isabel, she was possessed of an ardent, romantic nature and had a French mother, now dead.

During the winter months of early 1835, Herman left Pittsfield and joined his brother Gansevoort in the fur business. Now fifteen and a half, he kept the books of the firm for the following two years and assisted as a retail sales clerk in the flourishing Albany store. At some time during this period he enrolled as a student in the Albany Classical School. He also acquired membership in the Albany Young Men's Association, a club for debating and reading, of which his brother was already a member. Such clubs, in the absence of public libraries, were popular in many cities and served a most useful educational purpose.

In the latter half of 1836 a minor economic depression tricked Gansevoort Melville into the same financial whirlpool that had sucked in and broken his father. Suddenly, from those to whom he had extended credit, he found himself unable to collect sufficient cash to meet his obligations. In April, 1837, he was forced — like his father before him — into bankruptcy. That autumn, while Gansevoort went bravely about seeking to collect enough money from his debtors to salvage his business, Herman secured through Uncle Thomas a position as country schoolmaster in a small school near Pittsfield. Here he remained for a single term, returning to Albany at Christmas.

In February his efforts to reorganize a debating club, the Philo Logos Society, embroiled him in an extravagant argument with another member of the group in the pages of the *Albany Microscope*, a local gossip sheet.[7] That May, with Gansevoort ill and the family's fortunes at a low ebb, the Melvilles moved from Albany to the small neighboring town of Lansingburgh, where it was possible to live more thriftily. With some aid from Uncle Peter Gansevoort, they remained there in frugal circumstances for a number of years. Nobody suffered greatly from the change except Mrs. Melville, who considered nothing of quite so much importance as keeping up appearances.

After spending several weeks on his uncle's farm assisting with the harvest, Herman in early November, 1838, took steps to enter a new career. He thought there were prospects of a job on the Erie Canal and therefore undertook the study of surveying and engineering at the Lansingburgh Academy. Though this preparation increased his knowledge of science, it proved useless — in spite of his own efforts and those of his relatives — to secure him work. While, however, he was vainly pulling wires to snare a position in the surveying field, he wrote his first known literary compositions, which appeared under the pseudonym "L.A.V." in the *Democratic Press and Lansingburgh Advertiser* for May 4 and May 18, 1839. These amateurish "Fragments from a Writing Desk" are interesting only because they reveal something of his adolescent reading, his inclination toward the romantic in literature, and his unformed style.

II *Merchantman and Whaler*

Now nearly twenty, Melville faced a bleak future. He was without a steady job, unable to decide upon a career, and certainly unhappy about his lack of success in contributing to the support of a nearly destitute family. Gansevoort, striking out for himself, left in May for New York City to seek better opportunities and to read law. He took with him the younger brother Allan, who had been miserably earning a pittance in Uncle Peter's office. When the brothers departed, they made a promise to keep their eyes open for something that might interest Herman. A few days later Gansevoort wrote announcing that a berth had been located for him aboard a packet sailing the following week for Liverpool. Thus it was that when the three-masted *St. Lawrence,* under the command of Captain Oliver P. Brown, set sail from New York harbor on June 5, 1839, it carried on board as one of its crew members young Herman Melville, bound now on the first maritime adventure of his life.[8]

In the next four months Melville tasted what he was to describe in his books as the unexpectedly brutal and evil existence of sailors.

As a landlubber serving the ship in the position of mere "boy" or apprentice, he had to endure not only the usual rigors of sea life but the hazing to which the crew enjoyed subjecting a newcomer. Furthermore, his patrician air and his education, plus the fact that he was two or three years older than the general run of boys going to sea, no doubt encouraged greater sarcasm and practical joking at his expense. In any event, the voyage (doubtless beginning for Melville with the cleaning of the pigpens and chickencoops on deck that he was to speak of so ruefully in *Redburn*) seems to have proved more disillusioning than exciting. In about four weeks the *St. Lawrence* anchored in the harbor of Liverpool and remained there a month and a half discharging and loading cargo. Melville had ample time to acquaint himself with examples of the squalor and vice then prevalent around the docks. On August 13, the ship weighed anchor for its return voyage and reached New York at the end of September, docking there October 1.

His first voyage aroused in Melville no desire for a maritime career; he made no move to secure another berth but went home at once to Lansingburgh, where he found his family in direr straits than ever. His mother, who complained bitterly to her well-to-do brothers that they should be helping her more generously to keep the family together, was threatening to disgrace them by breaking up her home and sending the children to live with different relatives or anyone else willing to take them. Herman was able to add a little to the family income by teaching school at Greenbush, New York.

Not long after his return from the sea, Herman seems to have become romantically interested in Harriet Fly, the sister of his close friend, Eli Fly, with whom Melville later ventured West. Though almost nothing is known about the lady or the details of their association, her signature and comments appear in the book which Herman had received eight years before as a prize at the Albany Academy.[9] Soon difficulties arose respecting the budget and the teacher's salary at Greenbush; in fact, before the end of May the school closed for lack of money. Briefly Melville filled in as a teacher in the school at Brunswick, only a two-mile walk from his home.

He had meanwhile decided, like other young men of his day, to try his fortune in the West. Uncle Thomas had moved some time earlier to Galena, Illinois, a lead-mining town on the edge of the Great Prairie. With his chum Eli, Herman set out in June, 1840, to visit his uncle and to explore possibilities of establishing himself in some paying vocation there. The prospects proved wholly discouraging. Thomas, though prominent in civic affairs, had been powerless to recoup his fortunes; in addition, he found both his neighbors and the Illinois climate uncongenial. After an excursion up the Mississippi to the famous falls of St. Anthony, Herman and Eli took a steamer downstream to the Ohio River at Alton and headed for home with nothing gained but experience. The river voyage, however, provided Melville with a setting for his rambling satire, *The Confidence-Man.*

Late fall of 1840 found the two young men in the city of New York, where they had gone to look for work. In their search they were aided by Gansevoort, who was still engaged in the study of law. While Eli shortly found a suitable job, Herman's daily foraging produced nothing. He was at length driven to make one of those crucial decisions that shape men's destinies. By Christmas Day his plans were fully formed; and on January 3, 1841, when the whaling ship *Acushnet* out of Fairhaven, Massachusetts, with Captain Valentine Pease, Jr., in command, slipped her moorings in the New Bedford harbor and set sail for the South Seas, Melville was aboard her on what would prove to be for literature one of the most important voyages of all time.[10]

The route followed by the *Acushnet* in her maiden voyage to the South Seas fisheries — a voyage lasting from 1841 to 1845 — was not the same route that author Melville indicated later for the *Pequod*, Captain Ahab's vessel in *Moby-Dick*; nor were her crew and officers the counterparts of those on the fictional ship. The first few months of Melville's whaling experience were pleasant and propitious. After two months the *Acushnet* arrived at Rio de Janeiro and celebrated a successful start of the voyage by transferring 150 barrels of whale oil to a homeward-bound ship. Pausing only a day in the beautiful harbor, the *Acushnet* sailed southward for the Cape, rounding it a month later with no serious difficulty. In May the boats were lowered for whales in the Pacific opposite Valparaiso, the ship then proceeding northward until, on June 23, the anchor was dropped in the port of Santa, Peru. Here Melville wrote a letter home. In July the cruise continued as far north as the Galapagos Islands and then westward along the equator.

For eleven months in 1841 and 1842 the *Acushnet* sailed far and wide in its hunt for sperm whales through the favorite whaling grounds of the South Pacific. Unfortunately, luck was bad. Only a few whales were killed, and the hold in which the barrels of rendered oil were stored was filling all too slowly. Captain Pease, perhaps as the combined result of ill health and the poor catch, grew daily more irritable and short of temper. Later he was to quarrel violently with his first and third mates and impel them to leave the ship. Morale among the crew, noticeably high during the first months of the cruise, dropped now to a low pitch. When the *Acushnet* lowered its anchor in the quiet, peaceful harbor of Nuku Hiva in the Marquesas Islands to take on water and other supplies on June 23, 1842, Mellville apparently had swallowed his fill of the bad feeling then current on the ship and what he considered unwarranted cruelty on the part of the captain. Exactly when and how he formed his decision to desert is not known, though he was clearly strengthened in his determination by discovering similar thoughts in the mind of Richard Tobias Greene, a fellow crewman.

III *South Seas Adventure*

The events beginning on July 9, 1842, were to furnish the fascinating plot for Melville's first novel, *Typee.* Greene figures in the story under the name of Toby. Shortly before the ship was to sail, Melville and Greene, having informed themselves as much as they could about the island and its inhabitants, escaped inland by laboriously climbing the tall cliffs that surrounded the bay. They struck out for a valley occupied by the Happa tribe,[11] known to be friendly to white sailors. They planned to lie in hiding here until the ship's departure and then to live comfortably in Marquesan style for as long as pleased them. But they had not counted on the wild, hilly terrain of the interior and the impossibility of locating any familiar landmarks to guide them. After a day or two of struggling across rough and unpromising country, of resting little and eating almost nothing, they stumbled by miscalculation into the unfriendly territory of the Taipis (Typees), a fierce tribe of reputed cannibals. During the journey across the hills Melville suffered a mysterious injury or infection of the leg that annoyed him and occasionally incapacitated him for the next three months.

The Taipis, belying their savage reputation, admitted the two strangers to their villages with an outward show of hospitality. For a time the young Americans led an exciting, active, but comfortable and interesting life among their native hosts. As the days passed, however, their sojourn in the Taipi valley began to look more and more like a captivity. After a couple of weeks Toby was given permission to leave the valley in search of a doctor or medicines for Melville's ailing leg. He disappeared, and it was many months before his fate was learned: he had been impressed aboard a short-handed whaler then visiting the area to pick up stray crewmen. "Tommo," as Melville was called by the islanders, remained in the valley another two weeks, observing the native customs and constantly worrying about the risk of being eaten. He escaped at last through the help of men from the *Lucy Ann*, an Australian whaling barque. He always referred to his month among the Taipis with mixed feelings. While admiring the innocence of the natives and their unspoiled Rousseauesque existence and relishing his perhaps more than friendly association with the native beauty Fayaway, he also recalled his gnawing fear of becoming eventually the object of his hosts' cannibalistic tendencies.

On August 9, 1842, he fled back to the relative security of another whaling ship, but the situation on the *Lucy Ann* could hardly be termed an improvement over the one he had known on the *Acushnet*. Its captain proved incompetent and its mate a drunkard. Several members of the crew had recently deserted, and some were in irons aboard a warship for mutiny. When the ship called at Papeete in September to obtain medical attention for the captain, it remained just outside the harbor in order to discourage further desertions. Conditions on board were inspected by a physician, Dr. Francis Johnstone, and the acting British consul for Tahiti. It was agreed among these officials and the ship's officers that the *Lucy Ann* should be sent on a short whaling cruise under command of the first mate while the captain remained on shore to receive medical treatment.

Not long after the ship started this cruise it was forced back by the threat of open mutiny. Several troublesome sailors — among them the ailing Melville — were put ashore for trial as mutineers. Most of them escaped or were informally released in October from the loose confinement of the local calaboose. With John B. Troy, a demoted former surgeon who had been steward of the *Lucy Ann* and who appears as Dr. Long Ghost in Melville's novel *Omoo,* Melville now seized the opportunity to explore the widely known Broom Road along the shores of Tahiti and then crossed over to the neighboring island of Eimeo, where the two accepted work temporarily on a potato farm. By the end of October they were back on Tahiti, tramping along the beaches, examining some of the attractive and still uncivilized corners of the island, and looking for a spot where they would not be in danger of arrest.

At Papetoi, after sundry adventures later described in *Omoo*, Melville shipped — possibly as a harpooner — on the *Charles and Henry*, his third whaling ship, during the first week of November. The ship went south and then east, arriving near the end of January, 1843, near the coast of South America. Whales proved elusive, however; and when the ship came to anchor at Lahaina in the Hawaiian Island on April 26, it carried only a small cargo of whale oil. Melville collected his minute share of the profits and was officially discharged on May 2 at the end of what must have been for him an extremely agreeable voyage. A few days later he was in Honolulu, and here he placed his name on a contract for future work as clerk and bookkeeper in a new store soon to be opened by one of the local merchants.

In Honolulu his observations convinced him, if he had not been convinced before, that the "superior" classes coming from Europe and America to missionize and civilize the simple and honest South Sea islanders were actually despoiling and enslaving them instead. He would complain in his books that the islanders had been "civilized into draft horses, and evangelized into beasts of burden"; but the brutal frankness of such charges did little to win either belief or support from the influential missionary societies of his day. These allegations only resulted in turning readers against him.

IV   *The Navy*

Melville wrote home from Honolulu that he was planning to spend the whole of the next year there, but something caused him to change his mind. On August 17, 1843, he enlisted as an ordinary seaman aboard the frigate *United States,* a fine American warship, and only two days later set sail for home. Melville's next several months as a full-fledged member of the United States Navy provided the framework for *White-Jacket,* his man-of-war novel. One characteristic of naval tradition that impressed itself most sharply upon Melville's consciousness was the causeless brutality of its legal code. He was to dwell on this matter at some length in *White-Jacket,* in which he would single out for special condemnation official flogging, the time-honored punishment for minor transgressions.

On the *United States* he met in the line of his duties one of the greatly revered heroes of his life, Jack Chase. An Englishman with a bent for literature and adventure who delighted in quoting long passages from the *Lusiad,* John J. Chase had once deserted from the navy to fight on the side of Peru in its war against Bolivia. Pardoned because of his excellent record and known ability as a leader of men, he now served as captain of the maintop. He was Melville's immediate superior and constant companion throughout the voyage. The measure of Chase's personal and literary influence is indicated by Melville's making him the dedicatee of *White-Jacket.*

The frigate sailed in a leisurely course over portions of the Pacific already familiar to Melville. Stops were made at both Nuku Hiva and Tahiti. At Callao, Melville may have heard his first news of the *Somers* affair, a strange, dramatic incident in which three Americans (including Philip Spencer, son of the Secretary of War) had been hanged for mutiny after a courtmartial trial presided over by Melville's cousin, Lieutenant Guert Gansevoort. The event was to stick in Melville's mind and eventually be transformed into the plot for his posthumously published short novel, *Billy Budd.* After weeks of lying in port interrupted by a quiet excursion to Mexico for a supply of silver dollars, the *United States* at last resumed its way homeward in July, 1844. While the ship was turning Cape Horn, Melville may have made for himself the many-layered garment described in *White-Jacket* which gave that work its title. On October 3 the vessel dropped anchor in the Boston harbor; on October 14 the young wanderer drew his pay and was discharged from naval service.

V *The Search Ends*

In Lansingburgh the four years of Melville's absence had brought a degree of improvement in the family fortunes. The return of better times to the nation's economy, while not restoring former prosperity, had at least started the Melvilles toward financial and social recovery. Gansevoort had become a persuasive orator in the presidential campaign of James Polk. Allan, long the problem child of the family, was making good as a lawyer on Wall Street. Helen, the oldest sister, lived at home, still unmarried; her dearest friend and frequent visitor was Elizabeth Shaw, daughter of Judge Lemuel Shaw of the Supreme Court of Massachusetts who had been a close friend and confidante of her father.

Herman received a joyful welcome from his mother and sisters and before long was telling and retelling the spellbinding story of his adventures. One of those who listened most attentively was Elizabeth Shaw. In time, doubtless at the urging of his female relatives, Melville began to commit the account of his adventures to paper. The result was *Typee*. Brother Gansevoort, who had been appointed secretary of the legation in London as a reward for his campaign activities, arranged for publication of the book in London just before his illness and sudden death in May, 1846. In this country Melville made his own publishing arrangements.

Typee achieved immediate and startling success both in England and in America, and almost at once Melville began work on a sequel. The overnight popularity of his first offering in the field having demonstrated unequivocally his predilection for authorship, Melville now realized that he had unexpectedly discovered his true calling. Washington Irving, looking over the proof sheets in the legation office in London, pronounced the book a masterful accomplishment. John Murray, Melville's British publisher, was deceived into thinking it the work of a practiced professional writer.

His brother Thomas having chosen the sea for his career and departing on a voyage to the Pacific, Melville was left in charge of the family's financial affairs during the summer of 1846. Yet he managed by hard work to complete the manuscript of a second book, *Omoo,* before the end of the year. Like *Typee,* the book dealt romantically with his adventures in the South Seas and continued the tale from exactly where the first book had ended. Like *Typee,* it gave detailed and fascinating descriptions of the islanders, and with an even sharper and more accurate realism. When *Omoo* were published in the spring of 1847, complaints against the book were strongly registered by critics who mistrusted his rough treatment of the missionaries, but everybody agreed on its merit as an interesting story.

VI   *Family Man*

With two successful novels to his credit, Melville could well believe that authorship now promised the means by which he would make his fortune. Still, he was not willing to trust this activity alone as a source of income. He was thinking of getting married, a step for which he was poorly prepared financially. He had already chosen the girl; for the acquaintance with Helen's friend Elizabeth Shaw had blossomed, with his family's encouragement, into real affection. Using his brother's name and his own literary success as recommendations, he tried unsuccessfully to obtain appointment as a clerk in the Treasury Department in Washington. This attempt became the first of a long series of discouraging failures in the search for security. For two decades Melville was to continue his periodic applications to the federal government for a position to which he thought his abilities and family connections entitled him, but the effort was always in vain.

Among Melville's associates at this time the most influential in the field of literature was Evert Duyckinck, prominent New York editor and writer. As editorial adviser to Wiley and Putnam, he had been active in getting *Typee* ready for the press, had been editor of the *Arcturus* magazine, and was currently in charge of the *Literary World,* for which Melville wrote occasional reviews. With Duyckinck's coterie of writers, Melville subsequently helped in planning and writing for a short-lived comic weekly called *Yankee Doodle.* Since by the summer of 1847 he was hard at work on his third novel, however, Melville could spare only a little time for minor productions.

On August 4, with only such income in prospect as he could earn from his writings—an uncertain prospect at best—Melville married Elizabeth Shaw in Boston. After a wedding trip into upper New England and Canada made somewhat uncomfortable by the travel accommodations of the day, the newlyweds returned, and in September they settled with Herman's brother Allan and his new bride in a spacious house at 103 Fourth Avenue, New York City. The house was large enough not only for the two young couples but also for Melville's mother and unmarried sisters. Here, with some understandable congestion of people and activities, Melville carried on a pleasant social life and simultaneously put his energies into the task of making a living from his books. The years 1847 and 1848 were certainly among the happiest of Melville's entire life.

Important intellectual changes occurred within Melville during the writing of *Mardi.*[12] In this, his third book, which he very likely began as a sequel to the adventures described with such exciting detail in his earlier works, he steered his creative craft without warning into a realm of satire, fantasy, and philosophy. Perhaps this change occurred because the events of his cruise on the *Charles and Henry* had been too dull to make a good yarn, but clearly his book was also affected by the reading which had recently aroused his interest in philosophical subjects. In any case, *Mardi,* which appeared in the spring of 1849, starts as if it were a continuation of *Omoo* but changes into an involved allegory in which the hero, Taji, vainly searches through a symbolic archipelago of strange lands for an answer to the riddle of the universe. While a mixture of adventurous talespinning, languorous poetry, and semisatirical philosophizing, it presents allegorically Melville's observations on almost every phase of human behavior and speculation. It particularly raises questions regarding politics and religion. This type of book, requiring serious thought while seeming to present pure entertainment, held small appeal for contemporary American reading audiences, and Melville was denounced swiftly by the critics for having drifted off course. If he had the good sense to return at once, they told him, to the interesting, straightforward, and factual style of *Typee* and *Omoo,* he might yet save himself; otherwise he must prepare for literary doom. Thus *Mardi* proved neither a critical nor a financial success.

On February 16, before *Mardi* was published, the Melvilles had their first son, Malcolm, who was born in Boston where Elizabeth had gone to be near her parents. The birth of a son gave Melville joy but increased the urgency of a larger income. The failure of *Mardi,* catching him completely by surprise, dealt him a hard blow; he had produced what he confidently expected would be a best seller, only to see it fail miserably. In the struggle for financial stability, Melville forced himself to write what he frankly regarded as two mere potboilers. The first, *Redburn,* was a tale based upon his youthful voyage aboard the *St. Lawrence.* Having now learned what American readers of his day demanded, Melville wrote a book that would be sure to sell; it combined fact with fancy in a style sufficiently easygoing and charming to draw praise from nearly everyone who read it. Nevertheless, to its author the book never could be anything else than hack work. During the same year of 1849 that witnessed the publication of *Redburn,* Melville started a second bread-and-butter novel, *White-Jacket,* which relates the story of life on a man-of-war and roughly follows the outline of his voyage on the *United States.* It was ready to publish within a few months; but publication in America suffered a delay while Melville made a business trip to London to arrive at favorable arrangements for its publication there.

On this trip abroad he took the trouble to keep a journal which he doubtless felt might prove of use to him in preparing other stories or lectures.[13] He remained in London only long enough to complete the circuit of all the leading publishers and to pay a number of social calls before embarking on a hurried educational and pleasure tour of a part of the Continent. As always, he spent much time in old book shops. Though he knew that, as a writer, he should seize the opportunity to study British life in detail while he had the opportunity, he soon grew homesick and began penning yearning letters to his wife depicting his loneliness for her and the baby. He finished his negotiations with Richard Bentley for publication of *White-Jacket;* then at Christmastime, despite an unanticipated but flattering invitation to visit the duke of Rutland at Belvoir Castle in January, he resolutely took passage for home on a sailing vessel rather than a steamer in order to save expense.

CHAPTER 3

The White Whale Breaches

I Country Gentleman

WHEN MELVILLE reached New York City and gratefully disembarked on February 1, 1850, he had good reason to feel that his future as an author was entirely secure. *Typee* and *Omoo* still enjoyed a wide readership. Though *Mardi* had failed, both *Redburn* (which sold some 4,000 copies by February 16) and *White-Jacket* gave promise of strong popular appeal. He had been forming in his mind recently the plots of two other novels. One concerned the European adventures of Israel Potter, a soldier in the American Revolution, whose little book of supposed reminiscences (authentic or not) Melville had picked up some years before in his customary rummaging among quaint old book shops. The other, not yet so clearly worked out in his mind, was to offer an authoritative description of the great South Seas whaling industry and be embellished with incidents from his own experiences as a whaler. By March the second of these two books had begun to take definite shape.

Exactly the kind of work Melville had in mind when he first undertook the writing of what gradually and painfully grew into his masterpiece, *Moby-Dick,* is not easy to say. When he mentioned the project with hopeful enthusiasm to Richard Bentley, he called it a "romance of adventure founded upon certain wild legends of the Southern Sperm Whale Fisheries, and illustrated by the author's own personal experience, of two years or more, as a harpooner."[1] Obviously *Moby-Dick* eventually turned into something much more than this, and what it became resulted from several external circumstances that markedly influenced his life at this period.[2] One of the influences undoubtedly was his rereading of Shakespeare;

44

another was his discovery of Thomas Carlyle, whose *Heroes and Hero-Worship* and *Sartor Resartus* he combed through with deep interest. A third was the friendship of Nathaniel Hawthorne, whom he met on a vacation jaunt in the Berkshire Hills, and other influences might be mentioned as well.

In July and August Melville vacationed in Pittsfield, boarding at his cousin Robert's home (the house later named "Broadhall" — now the Pittsfield Country Club). He seems to have been searching for a piece of Berkshire property on which he could settle as a country squire — engaging in agriculture as a sideline but maintaining his economic and social position chiefly through literature. The double household in the city had become crowded and noisy; furthermore, Elizabeth required the relief of a less humid climate at certain seasons of the year when she suffered from hay fever. The quiet and spacious countryside, the drier air, and the spectacularly beautiful border of mountains in the Pittsfield area fulfilled all Melville's requirements. It had already attracted a number of other literary people: Oliver Wendell Holmes came here every summer, living in his luxurious "Holmesdale" at the outskirts of the village; and Hawthorne had ensconced himself snugly in his "little red house" near Lenox. Other frequenters of the region included Fanny Kemble, the famous actress, and G. P. R. James, the historical novelist.

Exhilarated by the pure air of Pittsfield and the magnificent views of the wooded hills that surrounded it, Melville grandly invited two of his New York friends, Evert Duyckinck and Cornelius Mathews, to visit him there. On the spur of impulse one day they joined a bevy of other literary folk in a picnic on the slopes of Monument Mountain. Among those who climbed the mountain that memorable fifth of August were Duyckinck, Holmes, Mathews, Melville, Hawthorne, Harry Sedgwick, David Dudley Field, and James T. Fields. Many in the party subsequently recalled with enthusiastic approval an occasion enlivened with bottles of cool champagne and hilarious entertainment provided by certain of the climbers. Melville, according to one report, "bestrode a peaked rock, which ran out like a bow-sprit, and pulled and hauled imaginary ropes" for the delectation of the group.[3]

There is a legend that Hawthorne and Melville sought shelter together in a cleft of rocks during a sudden thunderstorm and engaged in a mutually stimulating talk on philosophy and literature.[4] In some respects the meeting with Hawthorne appears to mark a turning point in Melville's career; it encouraged him, certainly, to pursue his bent in the direction of intellectual speculation and, in spite of *Mardi,* to do so without fear. The two men were drawn together by similar interests and opinions and almost immediately formed a friendship that, on Melville's side at least, endured for life.[5] Within a few days each was reading the other's books with mounting enthusiasm. Hawthorne, stretched out on the newly gathered hay in his barn, devoured his friend's recent novels; some years earlier he had gone through *Typee* and reviewed it favorably.[6] Melville for his part had already written an admiring review for *The Literary World* of Hawthorne's *Mosses from an Old Manse* which appeared on August 17 and 24; in it Melville had referred in glowing terms to Hawthorne as an American Shakespeare.

His acquaintance with Hawthorne gave Melville another good reason for settling in the Berkshires. On September 14, with help in the form of a large loan — the second — from his father-in-law to provide the down payment, Melville purchased the Brewster farm near Pittsfield for sixty-five hundred dollars. It contained 160 acres of land, a central-chimneyed house, reputed to have served once as a tavern, outbuildings, and a glorious view of Mount Greylock. The family occupied its new home at the beginning of October, and for a month Melville was kept busy with necessary repairs and farm work. Finding some Indian relics in one of his fields, he named the place "Arrowhead."

By winter he had nearly finished his book about whaling adventure. The stimulation of knowing Hawthorne, his own reading, and the mental ferment produced in Melville by the new life he was entering caused him to be dissatisfied, however, with what he had written. Aided by advice from his friend and fellow author Richard Henry Dana, he soon undertook the task of rewriting, adding, and revising.[7] Melville was at the height of his creative powers and furthermore in a state of considerable intellectual excitement. His work began to take a form unlike that of any other novel ever attempted; it combined wild adventure, heroic posturing, cetological description, and personal philosophical conjecture into an organic and artistic whole. His revisions took so much time that the manuscript he had expected to have ready by the end of 1850 did not reach the printer until the following autumn. *Moby-Dick* required nearly two years to write — longer than any of his works before or after it. Though there were many interruptions, it was his custom to write every day until well into the afternoon and, ruining his eyes in the process, to read and gather materials at night by lamplight. He spent the final months of composition and of revising, adding, and correcting printer's proof in a rented room near the Harper and Brothers building in New York.

Between chapters of the book he was occupied, of course, with a great many social activities and financial problems. There were visits from his own and Elizabeth's numerous relatives, excursions and parties with such congenial neighbors as the R. J. Morewoods (Mrs. Morewood was an indefatigable party-giver), and a highly agreeable visit by the Duyckinck brothers which included a mountain-climbing picnic on Mount Greylock and an all-night stay in the observatory at the summit. When the note held by Brewster for the remaining balance on "Arrowhead" fell due, Melville asked for an advance against royalties from his publisher. Since he had already dipped rather heavily into his account, however, the request was refused. He found it necessary to borrow over two thousand dollars at a substantial rate of interest in order to satisfy his obligations.

Moby-Dick sold well for several weeks after its publication in November,[8] but the critical reception of the book proved surprisingly varied — on the whole, it was rather disappointing than otherwise. Many critics gave the work unstinted praise; others regarded it as only another *Mardi*. Melville's greatest joy came from the reaction of Hawthorne, who seems to have understood at once the book's importance and bestowed his blessing. Mrs. Hawthorne also warmly commended the novel. The close personal and literary ties that Melville had woven between his own life and that of Hawthorne were unfortunately soon disrupted by the latter's removal from Lenox to Concord. From this time on the two men saw each other only infrequently.

II *Financial and Other Problems*

The lack of an income adequate for the style of living he coveted for his family still plagued Melville and forced him to continue writing. He had earned an average in royalties of some twelve hundred dollars for each of his first six books — not a princely sum even for those days. Through advances he had been able to secure about seven hundred dollars in cash for his expenses during the winter of 1851-1852; but by now his account with Harper and Brothers, his American publisher, had been overdrawn by more than four hundred dollars. With no income other than what he could earn from his farm and his writing, Melville by November was necessarily engrossed by another book — one he determined should contain the elements of drama, mystery, and sentiment calculated for quick popularity.

Pierre was to be a story that would appeal to feminine readers. Writing to Mrs. Hawthorne, Melville promised "a rural bowl of milk" without the masculine savagery of a *Moby-Dick*. There can be little doubt of his intention to imitate some of the sentimental tales of country life then so common in English and American literature. But in the composition his irrepressible habit of deep philosophical analysis asserted itself. In *Pierre* the handsome, talented, and wealthy hero tries to lead a life of perfect virtue. Discovering an apparent skeleton in the family closet and confronting the ethical problem that it suggests, he somehow turns every virtuous intention into evil consequences. The book is hardly the innocent country idyll that Melville promised; it is a searching study of the perplexing ambiguities of human behavior and moral law. In some of its aspects it may be regarded as a precursor of the psychological novel of today.[9]

Melville wrote the book under severe difficulties. Elizabeth, after the birth of Stanwix in October, 1851, had become nervous and irritable and was therefore unable for the time being to serve as his amanuensis. Her help in that capacity, as well as that of his adoring sister Augusta, had hitherto proved extremely valuable. Now Elizabeth, who had begun to worry audibly about the strain of overwork upon her husband, acted as if she wished, for his welfare, to delay the book as much as possible. Hawthorne was no longer at hand to provide stimulating companionship.

Richard Bentley in London, having lost money on books of Melville that he had previously published, refused *Pierre* as a bad risk; as a result, makeshift arrangements for its British publication had to be sought. Harpers advanced five hundred dollars for the new book in February, 1852, but evinced no enthusiasm over its chances of popularity. In April, Melville took his wife with him to New York and saw the book through the press. Critics in general condemned *Pierre* upon its publication as an impure book. The moral conventionalist Evert Duyckinck, who as a friend had scolded Melville roundly for what he regarded as immoral teachings in *Moby-Dick,* was horrified by its successor; he concluded that its author had actually gone mad. This virtually extinguished the friendship, which had been on the wane, of course, ever since Duyckinck's priggish attacks on the whaling masterpiece.

The need of respite from the cramping demands of steady writing and his temporary neglect of the farm caused Melville during May and June to spend nearly all his time out-of-doors. He hired a helper, plowed and planted his fields, and repaired his buildings. It was during this period that he erected on the north side of his house the famous piazza which furnished a title and sketch for *The Piazza Tales.* Later he accompanied his father-in-law, who shared Elizabeth's concern about her husband's health, on a court junket which took them to Nantucket and Martha's Vineyard islands. Though the opening scene of *Moby-Dick* is laid at Nantucket and the island's whaling history is woven into the tale, Melville had never before set foot there. On this excursion he heard the pathetic story of Agatha Robertson, who bore patiently her husband's desertion and his return years afterward with another wife. Melville sent the details of the affair to Hawthorne with an inscribed copy of *Pierre.* The latter expressed gratitude for the story idea but sent it back with an obvious question: "Why did not Melville himself use the story?"[10]

Melville, though more than a little disturbed and surprised by the unfavorable reaction to *Pierre,* had no thought of giving up his literary career.[11] On the other hand, his relatives were exerting strong pressure for him to do so because of worry over the effect of overwork on his health and because of dissatisfaction over the tiny income his writing produced. After the election of Franklin Pierce, Melville's family and friends made efforts to secure him a consular appointment. Even Hawthorne, a college chum of Pierce and his campaign biographer, joined in the attempt, but nothing came of it. In February, 1853, *Putnam's Monthly* publicized Melville in two articles written by Fitz-James O'Brien. Though generally complimentary, they warned Melville against the tendencies he had shown in *Pierre.* Melville continued writing steadily through the winter. In March he received a jarring financial report from Harper and Brothers revealing that, instead of having royalties due him, he was overdrawn by more than three hundred dollars.

If Melville's family had serious cause for its concern over the state of his health, one may guess that the reason lay less in the

physical and mental strain of overwork than in the crushing paucity
of expected financial rewards from his books and in the blasting of
his high hopes for literary recognition. Melville cannot in truth be
said to have suffered anything like poverty in these years: he had
money on deposit in the Pittsfield bank; he was able to earn enough
out of his farm profits to make additional deposits at intervals; and
his wife enjoyed a moderate income from a trust fund. Melville
nevertheless appears to have considered himself poor, and he
complained about his financial troubles in his correspondence with
Hawthorne — a man who had experienced actual penury and could
thus have had scant sympathy for a gentleman-farmer with so
many rich relatives. Although Melville certainly had no real fears
of going "to the Soup Societies" for aid,[12] his bitterness at the
critical reception of both *Moby-Dick* and *Pierre* cannot be
doubted. He was disappointed by the American public's plain lack
of perceptiveness. For some time after 1852 one finds in his
writings a peculiar preoccupation with characters who are happy
failures or who retain their pride and integrity in the face of
undeserved misfortune.

III   *Magazine Writer*

Melville never used the "Agatha" plot which Hawthorne had
returned to him, but in 1853 he began to write a variety of tales and
short sketches for periodicals. The earliest of these were stories of
dignified patience like "Bartleby the Scrivener," which appeared in
Putnam's for November–December, 1853, and "Cock-a-Doodle-
Doo!" published by *Harper's* in December of the same year. He
agreed with Harper and Brothers to prepare a book on tortoises
and tortoise hunting based in part on his observations of the
Galapagos Islands, but this work was never finished, even though
he received an advance of three hundred dollars on the strength of
his proposals. The materials he prepared for it presumably became
the group of sketches entitled "The Encantadas or Enchanted
Islands," printed in *Putnam's* from March through May, 1854.

The editor of *Putnam's* refused a satrical sketch of Melville's
çalled "The Two Temples" because of its too strongly suggested
criticism of New York's newly opened Grace Church. In it a shab-
bily dressed man is turned away from services in a fashionable new
church, but he finds joy in the less respectable, not so sanctimon-
ious atmosphere of a public theater. A somewhat similar sketch,

"Poor Man's Pudding and Rich Man's Crumbs," was accepted by *Harper's* for its June issue. Meanwhile, Melville had been rewriting in an interesting style the narrative of Israel Potter, a soldier of the Revolution who had spent years in captivity abroad before coming home to be greeted by the neglect and ingratitude of his fellow countrymen. This very readable narrative began to run in *Putnam's* in July, 1854, and was published in book form in March, 1855. In the issue containing the second installment, *Putnam's* also printed "The Lightning-Rod Man," a satire on the conflict between human fear and man's trust in God, suggestive of episodes in Melville's later book, *The Confidence-Man. Harper's* in July and August, 1854, carried a pair of Melville's tales, "The Happy Failure" and "The Fiddler" — the first about an inventor who did not learn contentment until his prized invention failed, the second about a child prodigy on the violin who won fame in early life but spent his adult years in happy obscurity.

In October, Melville received from Harper and Brothers a full report of the loss which had occurred in the famous fire of the previous winter that had wiped out nearly the entire stock and records of the company. Some twenty-three hundred of Melville's volumes, both bound and in sheets, had added their fuel to the blaze. To complicate his financial problems, Melville still owed the publisher a debt for advance royalties of three hundred and twenty dollars. To meet his financial obligations and in spite of increasing signs of exhaustion, he bent all his efforts during the cold months of that winter and spring to the continued production of tales and sketches. "The Paradise of Bachelors and the Tartarus of Maids," an indirect attack upon conditions in the New England mills with sex symbolism that was over the heads of most readers, appeared in *Harper's* for April, 1855. During the time that he was working on "Benito Cereno," one of his most controversial stories, an attack of rheumatism rendered him practically helpless for several days, and the prospect of spring plowing and planting with a stiff, sore back no doubt occasioned him great anxiety.

Though a handful of critics have proclaimed "Benito Cereno" a bore, the majority classify it with the finest of the world's literature. Melville stole the plot of "Benito Cereno" without acknowledgment from Amasa Delano's *Narrative of Voyages and Travels* (1817); but he skillfully transmuted it into a dramatically intense and symbolically suggestive mystery of the sea. Captain Delano in 1805 had met, under odd circumstances, the *Tryal,* a Spanish slaver, off the coast of Chile. Discovering that she was manned by slaves, who had overcome the officers and crew in a shrewdly planned and well-executed revolt, the American captain had captured the ship and sailed her to port, where the rebels had been tried and condemned. With numerous changes in the plot that heighten the suspense and symbolism, "Benito Cereno" appeared in *Putnam's* in three installments, beginning in October, 1855. Some critics maintain that Melville began the work as a novel but left it in abbreviated form in order to secure needed cash quickly. The writing, in any case, must have been slow and physically painful; for during most of 1855 Melville was far from a well man. Farm work became impossible for long periods of time, and it was probably during this year (marked also by the birth of a daughter, Frances) that he began to consider the advisability of moving back to the city. In this line of thinking he was no doubt encouraged by his wife, who hated Pittsfield winters.

All the sketches and stories written by Melville at this ambivalent stage of his career contain more than a smattering of symbolism and philosophical digression. "The Bell-Tower," a somewhat melodramatic tale of a clockmaker killed by his own invention, suggests the dangers implicit in the scientific and mechanical progress of the ninteenth century — a movement just then entering its heyday. This kind of writing, representing a point of view that was rapidly becoming outdated, could add little or nothing to his popularity. It made the editors of *Putnam's*, in which the story appeared, begin to insist that he put his talents to better and more profitable use by producing, instead of such deep-diving intellectual stuff, another "good" narrative of adventure. If he had been able at this juncture to write another *Typee* or *Omoo,* everyone concerned — perhaps even Melville himself — would have been overjoyed.

Continued ill health plagued him throughout the spring and summer. In June he came down with sciatica; and his neighbor Dr. Oliver Wendell Holmes was called in to examine him. His illness induced fits of moodiness, resulting finally in a decision to sell his property and abandon farming. When a local commission was given the task of selecting a location for a lunatic asylum, he promptly invited them to look over "Arrowhead," but it was found unsuitable for the purpose.

Despite his illness and continued sense of frustration, he succeeded in writing for *Putnam's* one of the most charmingly personal of his brief sketches, the good-natured but variously interpreted "I and My Chimney" (March, 1856). In it, the main interest centers around the enormous chimney at "Arrowhead" and the family's attempts to destroy it in order to improve the architecture of the house. The chimney, like Melville himself in his resistance to pressure from his relatives urging him to choose a career less exacting and more highly remunerative than authorship, holds out against every attack. At the end of the sketch the narator is able to say, with evident satisfaction, "I and my chimney, we smoke together" — an assertion of proud independence in the control of his own destiny.

He welcomed news from the Harpers that plans were under way for reissuing several of his books, and his health gradually improved. By the end of autumn, 1855, he was again attending social functions, including a fancy dress picnic at which his wife won the prize for the best costume. But despite these improvements, he wrote more stories of misfortune such as "Jimmy Rose," printed in *Harper's* for November, in which a formerly wealthy gentleman, after being forced into bankrupt obscurity for a quarter of a century, resumes his previous cheerful nature in spite of his poverty. At the end of the year Melville neglected his farm work while he applied himself to writing the last of the novels published within his lifetime, *The Confidence-Man,* which describes a steamer voyage down the Mississippi River. In it a cynical confidence man, assuming several different guises, cheats the gullible passengers while preaching the philosophy of charity and trust. The work, probably intended for serialization in *Putnam's,* pokes bitter fun at the inconsistencies of human nature. While working on it, Melville wrote other short pieces and prepared a collection of them for publication in book form. *Harper's* published in March, 1856, "The 'Gees," a sketch about sailors of Portuguese descent. "The Apple-Tree Table," which appeared in *Putnam's* that May, is based on a true incident occurring in Williamstown, Massachusetts; an amazing insect, presumably deposited as an egg in a living apple tree, developed years later into adulthood and ate its way to the surface after the wood of the tree had been fashioned into a table.

IV   *Another Voyage*

In April Melville sold half his farm for fifty-five hundred dollars.

He still retained eighty acres of cleared fields, woods, and gardens. Part of the eight thousand dollars he now had on deposit in the bank he began to invest in stocks. He also collected his short pieces, entitled them *The Piazza Tales*, and these were published by Dix and Edwards in May, 1856. But by the time *The Confidence-Man* was ready for publication that autumn, Lizzie was again volubly worrying about her husband's health. Perhaps even more she was voicing her own sense of semiimprisonment, especially during the cold, snowy winters at Pittsfield. Lizzie by this time seems to have had more than enough of country life and was eager to move back to the city. She arranged with her father the loan of a large sum of money (to be charged in the future against inheritance) to send Herman away on a voyage that it was hoped might restore his health. Such a voyage might also serve to draw him away from his unprofitable career as author. As for the children, during Melville's absence the older ones could be cared for by various relatives while the younger ones accompanied Lizzie to Boston. It was in this way that Melville achieved his long-cherished wish to visit the Mediterranean and the Holy Land.

He had now reached the age of thirty-seven. In the struggle to maintain his family's position in society and to win his own in literature, he had come close to wearing himself out; he was tired and badly needed a change. While not an utter failure, he knew that what he felt impelled to write would not sell; moreover, his relatives, though proud of his ability to produce books, decried the meager financial rewards of authorship and were eager to have him find a career that would pay. In any case, when Melville left Pittsfield on September 27, 1856, he carried with him a manuscript copy of *The Confidence-Man* for possible sale abroad; and he parted from a family which had hopes of changing his career during his trip.

Melville stopped first at the little town of Gansevoort, New York, where he deposited young Stanwix for safekeeping and bade goodby to the matriarch of the family, Grandmother Melville. Sister Augusta and Lizzie remained behind at "Arrowhead" for a few days to close up the house. Upon reaching New York, Melville had the good sense to look up his former associate Evert Duyckinck and to renew their lapsed friendship. He also completed final negotiations with Dix and Edwards for the American edition of *The Confidence-Man*. After a splendid farewell dinner given for him by Daniel Shepherd, his brother Allan's one-time law partner and a fellow author,[13] Melville set sail on the steamer *Glasgow* on October 11.

The voyage may well have been as much a quest for faith as a journey for health. Certainly *The Confidence-Man* betrays the cynicism which had crept into his mind; even the intended humor of the book is darkened by the edge of bitterness. Now the relaxing air of the sea brightened his outlook. He kept a sketchy journal of his trip that would supply him with future literary materials.[14] After arrival in Glasgow, he saw the customary sights there and in Edinburgh; he then traveled on to Liverpool, perhaps by way of London, for a long-anticipated visit with Hawthorne. The latter, upon election of Pierce to the presidency, had received appointment as consul at Liverpool and had amassed a comfortable bank account from consular fees. The two old Berkshire neighbors, after some preliminary awkwardness, revived their warm feelings of earlier days and enjoyed on the beach at Southport an intimate and lengthy talk about "Providence and futurity, and of everything that lies beyond human ken."[15] Hawthorne found it surprising that his friend had altered so little since their last previous meeting, that he still displayed the same gravity of manner, the same disregard for fashion in clothing, the same predilection for philosophical and religious discussion. "If he were a religious man," Hawthorne remarked in his personal journal, "he would be one of the most truly religious and reverential; he has a very high and noble nature, and better worth immortality than most of us." Because Mrs. Hawthorne was in poor health, Melville did not pause long with the Hawthornes but shortly took passage for Constantinople. He left his trunk in Liverpool, traveling with only a carpet bag, and vested in Hawthorne authority to act for him in arranging British publication of *The Confidence-Man*. Though he was feeling better, Melville saw ruefully that the old spirit of adventure had gone out of him. Nevertheless, when the ship entered the Mediterranean and the November weather turned warm, he began to cheer up noticeably. He visited Malta and Greece, wondering at its masses of aimlessly swarming humanity and its colorful mixture of races. In December he embarked for Alexandria. Egypt impressed him with its dusty age, but his awe was reserved for the pyramids. When he climbed with difficulty to the top of one and gazed out over the broad scene below, he was filled, he said, with the sense of an ageless and brooding mystery.

He began his tour of the Holy Land early in January, 1857, when he landed at Jaffa and at once proceeded to Jerusalem. He saw the usual tourist attractions: Jericho, the Dead Sea, Bethlehem. What struck him, contrary to expectation, was the dull barrenness and unfruitfulness of this land of the Gospel; its atmosphere seemed not godly but somehow diabolic. Among those he met in his tour (including several Americans), many were to appear under other names in his narrative poem, *Clarel*. Departing from the unattractive "ecclesiastical countries" at the end of the month, Melville revisited Greece, made his way to Italy, and arrived in Rome on February 24. Although the cold weather brought him chest pains and kept him indoors for the best part of a month, he made a special effort to see the most famous buildings and statues.

After covering hastily the "grand tour" of northern Italy, he entered Switzerland and pressed on to Germany and Holland. From Rotterdam he took ship for London, landing there on April 26. After learning that, through Hawthorne's good offices, *The Confidence-Man* had been published by Longman's[16] and after seeing Madame Tussaud's waxworks and a few other spots of interest, he went on to Liverpool, glimpsing Oxford and the Shakespeare country on his way. On May 5, having paid a farewell call on Hawthorne and picked up his trunk, he sailed for home, weary and a little homesick, on the *City of Manchester*.

In his absence his relatives had been trying to prevent the likelihood of his falling back into his past routine by finding a position for him in the New York customs — but without avail. He felt good in mind and body upon his return and seems to have been ready to start a new book — from which his relatives dissuaded him — about his travels. But to celebrate his return his father-in-law gave an elaborate literary dinner at which two of the guests were Oliver Wendell Holmes and Richard Henry Dana, Jr. Then one of a group laying plans for the *Atlantic Monthly*, Holmes invited Melville to be a contributor.[17] The invitation was accepted verbally, though Melville begged off later. Meanwhile, *The Confidence-Man* had been received more favorably in England than in America; nowhere, however, did it sell in large quantities. Dix and Edwards, the firm which owned *Putnam's Monthly* and had published his two most recent books, went out of business in 1857 during the economic depression.

V *Lecturer and Office Seeker*

Melville now faced the task of earning a livelihood without a publisher. Advertising his farm for sale, he decided to try the lecture circuit. For some speakers this activity paid well, and Melville corresponded with George William Curtis,[18] a seasoned lecturer, to learn all he could about the business. By September he had scheduled some lectures for an average fee of fifty dollars and chosen a topic, "Statues in Rome."[19] Beginning on November 23 at Lawrence, Massachusetts, he gave the lecture in sixteen cities, the last of them being New Bedford, the great whaling port. While newspaper accounts indicated no special enthusiasm for Melville as a lecturer, most of the comments were at least politely commendatory. Although a neophyte in this field, Melville attracted fairly large audiences; and his family felt pleased because public speakers in the 1850's commanded more prestige than authors of slow-selling books. Not long after completing the lecture season and visiting his mother in Gansevoort, Melville began to complain of a severe "crick in the back," from which he was to continue suffering for several years. In September, despite spells of ill health, he looked, according to his friend George Duyckinck, robust and healthy; and secretly he had begun a new book — this time a book of poetry.[20]

Having netted about four hundred and twenty-four dollars during the first lecture season, Melville again advertised himself in 1858 as available to speak on a new topic, " The South Seas." Audiences undoubtedly would be eager to see in person "the man who had lived among the cannibals." He opened the second season in Yonkers, New York, on December 6; lectured in cities of the Midwest and also in his home town of Pittsfield; and fulfilled ten engagements in all for net earnings of five hundred and eighteen dollars. The following autumn, having failed in arranging for publication of his poetry, he lectured on "Traveling" but had only three engagements. His health, lack of interest in his lectures, or the economic recession of that period — several sponsoring organizations dropped or curtailed their programs[21] — may have caused the sudden end of his lecturing career. He was left with little to do, and again his family encouraged him to undertake a sea voyage. His brother Thomas was to sail in May, 1860, as captain of the clipper ship *Meteor*, bound for San Francisco and the Pacific Ocean. Melville accepted the invitation to sail as the captain's guest.

Before leaving, he deeded all his remaining property to Judge Shaw in return for cancellation of all his notes and made other arrangements that resulted in his being, for once, totally free of debt. The judge obligingly signed over the deeds to Lizzie, thus placing all Melvilles's holdings in his wife's name. Before he sailed on May 28, Melville hopefully entrusted to his brother Allan's care a volume of poetry and gave Allan instructions to find a publisher. On shipboard, foregoing his usual strenuous activity such as climbing high into the rigging, Melville contented himself with enjoying the ocean scenery, studying the ship's navigation, and writing a little poetry. The San Francisco newspapers took note of his arrival in that port and even hinted at his being persuaded to lecture, but Melville was not in the mood for such an effort; he felt homesick and weary. When the *Meteor's* orders were changed and he faced a long layover in San Francisco, he decided to return home. Taking a steamer to Panama, he crossed the Isthmus and embarked for New York early in November. His growing uneasiness was not improved upon his return when he learned that Allan had been unsuccessful in finding a publisher for the poems.

His relatives now urged him to seek a consular appointment under the newly elected President Lincoln. This time Melville fell in enthusiastically with their plans; and, encouraged particularly by a formal recommendation signed by several prominent citizens of Pittsfield, he journeyed in March, 1861, to Washington to see the President and to place his application in the hands of Senator Charles Sumner. The possibility of a post in Glasgow offered itself; but, while Melville was considering whether to have Sumner present his name or to wait for a better opportunity, he received word from home of the serious illness of his father-in-law. Starting back at once, he anxiously hurried with Lizzie to Boston. But Judge Shaw was already dead. The judge's estate of over fifteen thousand dollars, when divided among the heirs, gave Herman and Lizzie with their portion a security they had not known for a long while, and it enabled them to spend their next winter in the city rather than in the semiisolation of "Arrowhead."

In April, 1861, the firing upon Fort Sumter caught up all personal interests in the nationwide holocaust of war. Like other citizens, Melville followed the events of the capital and the camps with intense concern; in fact, he made use of these events in the poetry he was writing. He was ill with rheumatism during much of the winter in New York, but he was happy to mingle again in a more active world. Returning to Pittsfield in April, 1862, he made further efforts to dispose of "Arrowhead." By November he made up his mind that he would move to the city whether he sold the farm or not. On November 7, while moving furniture in his farm wagon, he had an accident which endangered his life: his horse bolted and threw him from the wagon to the ground. His friend J. E. A. Smith, editor of the *Berkshire Eagle,* who had been helping Melville, also fell to the ground but sustained only minor bruises. Melville's injuries included a broken shoulder blade and a number of cracked ribs. Attended by two physicians, he recovered slowly, his recuperation being complicated by attacks of neuralgia. One result of the accident was to make him for a time alarmingly indrawn and moody.

His troubles with regard to "Arrowhead" were at length solved when he traded it (with some additional capital) for his brother Allan's New York residence at 104 East 26th Street. An inheritance from his Aunt Priscilla provided him with funds to make repairs on the new quarters. Just prior to leaving Pittsfield permanently, Melville took part in the semicentennial celebration of the Albany Academy; he sat at the speaker's table as one of its distinguished alumni.

CHAPTER 4

Return to Native Grounds

I Gentleman and Poet

MELVILLE'S RETURN to the city of his birth was accomplished without further mishap during the autumn of 1863, and the winter was consumed in repairing and redecorating the house. Although he had no regular income other than interest from his investments and, of course, his wife's legacy, Melville appears to have lived in his New York home rather comfortably. He kept up social appearances, and he sent the children to good schools. By February, 1864, he was able to pay back to Harper and Brothers the sum of two hundred dollars, representing advance royalties long overdrawn on his account. This payment in a sense marked the close of his career as a novelist; henceforth he was to publish almost nothing except poetry.

The war held his close attention, and his poetry continued to reflect the accounts of battles and personalities given in the newspapers. During the spring when he and Allan, like many other civilians, made up their minds to examine at first hand the conditions under which the soldiers were fighting, they secured through Sumner a pass to visit the Army of the Potomac. Part of their object was to see their cousin, Colonel Henry Gansevoort, and they may have called on General Grant. Melville made such a good impression on the officers and men by his genuine interest and quick understanding that upon one occasion he was permitted to accompany a scouting party on its excursion into enemy territory. The experience of seeing the preparations for battle and the conditions of life in the war proved for Melville highly stimulating and provided materials for several poems,[1] though he came home from

the front with a savage attack of neuralgia that incapacitated him
for days.

Two other incidents of importance occurred that spring of 1864.
A family friend left Lizzie a legacy of three thousand dollars, which
paid off all outstanding debts on the house and supplied a small
cash reserve. In May came news of the death of Hawthorne, and it
was probably at this time that Melville wrote the moving poem entitled "Monody" to memorialize the deep attachment between
them:

> To have known him, to have loved him
> After loneness long;
> And then to be estranged in life,
> And neither in the wrong;
> And now for death to set his seal —
> Ease me, a little ease, my song!
>
> By wintry hills his hermit-mound
> The sheeted snow-drifts drape,
> And houseless there the snow-bird flits
> Beneath the fir-trees' crape:
> Glazed now with ice the cloistral vine
> That hid the shyest grape.

In 1865 a pirated edition of *Israel Potter,* published in Philadelphia as *The Refugee*, aroused his indignation and caused him to
write a strongly worded letter of protest. In the following year,
Melville's war poetry ultimately reached a pitch of quality as well as
timeliness that attracted more legitimate publishers. The Harpers
expressed willingness to print a few of the poems in the pages of
their magazine to test public reaction. In February, 1866, *Harper's*
carried "The March to the Sea"; it was followed in later issues by
"The Cumberland," "Philip" (renamed "Sheridan at Cedar
Creek"), "Chattanooga," and "Gettysburg." To Melville's amaze-
ment, even his relatives waxed enthusiastic over these pieces; and
the general response was auspicious enough to encourage further
production. In August *Battle-Pieces and Aspects of the War*, a collection of the war poetry, was published by Harper and Brothers. It
never became a popular success, nor did its forward-looking political and social ideas (such as his plea for the brotherhood of North
and South) exert any influence upon current affairs. It was, however, a thoroughly respectable piece of work, better calculated for

the approval of genteel readers and his own immediate circle than anything he had previously written.

The fact that his poems could be regarded as both patriotic and noncontroversial may have aided Melville in qualifying for appointment as deputy inspector of customs for the port of New York. A political scandal had forced a shake-up in the department's personnel, and the new collector, Henry Smythe, needed men of loyalty and probity for its reorganization. Melville had met Smythe in Switzerland and, upon hearing of his apointment, applied to him directly and was hired. He took his oath of office on December 5, 1866.

II Deputy Inspector of Customs

At forty-seven Melville was entering the only permanent paying job of his entire life. Though not a position of great responsibility or of social distinction, it gave him a regular schedule and it also benefited his health by taking him outside the house every day. The income of four dollars daily supplemented modestly his income from other sources. He enjoyed the work, and he could always do a little writing in his spare time.

His domestic life at this period, however, was far from a happy one. He had grown increasingly silent and withdrawn at home, not only because of his literary defeats but because of his frequent bouts with illness. He had turned moody over the years. Lizzie, though obviously not an easy person to live with and never known as a well-organized household manager, had complained for a long time to her immediate relatives about Herman's treatment of her. She even consulted her minister at the All Souls Unitarian Church to ask his advice on securing a marital separation.[2] The matter seems to have been urged on most vigorously by Lizzie's half-brother, Samuel S. Shaw, who regarded Melville as palpably insane. Whether the fault lay in Herman or Lizzie, the Melvilles in 1867 were close to a breakup as man and wife. That the separation did not occur was due partly to Lizzie's reluctance at making the crucial decision and partly to a tragic event in the autumn of that year which may have served the purpose of drawing them closer together.

The children in 1867 were beginning to approach maturity. Malcolm, eighteen in February, held a promising position with an insurance company. Passing through adolescence during the war years, he had formed romantic notions of military glory and had enlisted in a voluntary army group as soon as he reached the minimum age. Mixing with other young men of spirit, he acquired the habit of keeping late hours — a habit for which his father firmly berated him, finally taking away his house key — and of carrying a loaded pistol which he placed under his pillow at night. On September 10, Malcolm stayed out until three o'clock in the morning and had to be let in by his mother, who had waited up for him. In the morning he did not rise at his accustomed hour; his father, to teach him a lesson, deliberately allowed him to sleep so that he would be late for work. Although Malcolm responded in the morning to a call from his sister, nothing more was heard from him during the remainder of the day. In the evening, when he did not answer to repeated knocking, his father at length broke down the locked bedroom door and found Malcolm lying dead in his night clothes, the pistol in his hand and a bullet hole through his temple. The coroner's jury, first rendering a verdict of suicide, later altered this to "accidental self-destruction." Malcolm's death horribly affected both Herman, who had been too strict, and Lizzie, who had been overindulgent.

Within the year Melville's younger brother Tom retired from the sea and was elected governor of the Sailors Snug Harbor at nearby Staten Island. Troubled now and then by a "kink in his back," Melville probably gave little time to writing between 1867 and 1870, but he maintained his friendly contacts with the Duyckinck brothers and other literary acquaintances. When invited by the new editors of *Putnam's* to become a contributor, he gave his half-hearted promise to comply, but the effort proved more than he was willing to make. He was writing now mainly for personal satisfaction and entirely in verse.

During January, 1870, the disturbing news reached him that his younger son Stanwix, who had gone to sea, was reported as a deserter. The boy turned up in London, however, none the worse for wear and in July made a triumphant appearance at his grandmother's house in Boston. It was during this year that Melville, at the urging of his favorite brother-in-law, John C. Hoadley, sat for the splendid portrait of him by Joseph Eaton.[3] In February, 1872, Melville's brother Allan suddenly died of tuberculosis; in April he lost his aged mother and made the sad journey to Albany with her body for the burial. Stanwix, restless and unstable, perhaps unwisely petted by his parents after the death of Malcolm, constituted a continual source of worry. He had worked in his Uncle Allan's law office, shipped on a cruise around the world, gone to Kansas for a job in the harvest, attempted briefly to establish himself as a dentist, and undergone some hair-raising adventures in Central America. In 1873 he unexpectedly sailed away to California for two years of herding sheep.

"Proud, shy, sensitively honorable" Melville — as John Hoadley called him — led an uneventful existence during these later years; he conscientiously performed his duties at the custom house, often visited the Berkshire Hills or the White Mountains on vacation, but gave little attention to persons outside his own family. He underwent several spells of poor health and suffered from eyestrain, and the latter ailment clearly suggests that for some time he had been working on another book.

III *Poet of the Holy Land*

Clarel, his long poem about the Holy Land, was not completed until 1875. Its publication was paid for by Melville's generous and admiring uncle, Peter Gansevoort, who had long wanted him to write a book of this kind. After a vacation trip to Gansevoort and Pittsfield, in the course of which he had occasion to describe the poem to his uncle, Melville received a check for twelve hundred dollars to cover the cost of publishing it in book form. On the same day that arrangements for publication were completed, a telegram reached Melville reporting his uncle's death. The last weeks prior to its publication had been saddened for Melville by the death of his favorite sister Augusta, always his most faithful and affectionate admirer.

To Lizzie, who copied the manuscript for the printer, the book represented nothing but irritation and unhappiness. Because of it she had to cancel two previously scheduled visits from relatives. Furthermore, in the supervision of her work her husband proved impatient and demanding; the strain of proofreading took its toll on them both. *Clarel: A Poem and Pilgrimage in the Holy Land,* was not a book destined for popularity. Its 18,000 lines contained the bare skeleton of a plot fleshed out with Melville's reflections on religion, science, geography, and human conduct. Like *Mardi,* it concerns a journey and a search — the odyssey of the human mind in quest of certainty — but it lacks the variety and sparkle of his earlier work. Without Uncle Peter's financial help, the poem would have had little chance of being published. Issued in two volumes in June, 1876, it proved a puzzle to its readers and a soporific to the critics. It added nothing to its author's literary reputation except among his relatives.

A short biographical sketch by Melville about his Uncle Thomas appeared in J. E. A. Smith's history of Pittsfield in 1876. The writing of this and *Clarel* apparently reawakened Melville's interest in his former literary acquaintances, notably Evert Duyckinck. After several years of neglecting them, he again found considerable pleasure in their company and conversation. Sometimes he joined them at entertainments given by the Century Club, of which his brother Allan had been an active member. Among his dearest friends were Peter Gansevoort's daughter and son-in-law, Catherine and Abraham Lansing. Most of those who knew Melville in the 1870s appear to have regarded him as a frustrated genius who had never been given the chance to create the work of which he was really capable. Financially he was able to support his family in comfort and unquestioned respectability, but security had not been achieved without a struggle nor defended without threats of disaster. During one of the periodic investigations into irregularities in the affairs of his department in the customs, he barely escaped from the resulting wholesale dismissals. While his own innocence was never in question, his integrity did not save him from worry and fright.

In the spring of 1878, Melville suffered his first siege of erysipelas, a disease which deprived him temporarily of the use of his hands. Lizzie seems to have been made increasingly miserable by her chronic hay fever and other infirmities, though even more by the mental and physical ill health of her husband. During these years their life witnessed many changes. In 1877 Henry B. Thomas, recently from Philadelphia, began to call more or less regularly on Melville's younger daughter Frances (called Fanny) and married her in April, 1880. Elizabeth (Bessie) suffered at intervals from arthritis and in 1884 had such a severe attack of "muscular rheumatism" that for a time her life was despaired of. The death of Melville's brother Thomas in 1884 and of Lizzie's brother Lemuel a few weeks later made Melville begin to feel old. He found some solace in growing roses. Carefully cultivating a superb garden, he enjoyed giving bouquets to his closest friends.

But Melville shunned the younger literary men and curiosity seekers who occasionally sought him out. Four of his books —

Omoo, Redburn, White-Jacket, and *Moby-Dick* — still remained in print and were being read by a coterie of readers in the United States and Britain. Some British writers, especially W. Clark Russell and Robert Buchanan, publicly praised Melville's works and asked why Americans did not recognize him as one of their great authors.[4] Between Melville and the public in this country there had grown over the years an attitude of mutual indifference.

On the death of Lizzie's stepmother and stepbrother, she fell heir to substantial funds that enabled her to allocate the sum of twenty-five dollars per month to her husband for the purchase of books and prints. A number of other gifts and bequests were settled on Melville by relatives, making the salary earned at the custom house no longer necessary to him. In December, 1885, having completed nineteen years of honorable service, he retired gratefully to the relaxation of private life. Now nearly sixty-seven, tired from the long economic struggle and the suppression of his literary ambitions, Melville for a time simply rested. But early in 1886 came the disheartening news that Stanwix, after a prolonged illness, had reached the end of his tragic life in a San Francisco hospital. Melville took the tidings with a numbed resignation; Lizzie, however, never entirely recovered from the shock.

IV   *The Final Years*

Quietly Melville set himself the task of putting into a semblance of order the reams of unpublished or unfinished writings which he had accumulated over the years. Three separate volumes of his fragments, both poetry and prose, took shape in his mind.[5] One of these, a collection of miscellaneous pieces dealing chiefly with old sailors, he published privately in 1888 in an edition of only twenty-five copies under the title of *John Marr and Other Sailors.* Its dedication paid the author's respects to the popular British writer of sea stories, W. Clark Russell. During the year of its publication Melville made a short vacation voyage to Bermuda and Florida, with so rough a passage home that he could cross the deck only by crawling on hands and knees.

At about this time, if not earlier, Melville began to nourish in his mind the germ of a story about a handsome young sailor named Elisha Small who had been hanged for mutiny a long time before aboard the brig-of-war *Somers.* Just before dropping to his death from the yardarm, Small had astounded the witnessing officers and crew by exclaiming, "God bless the flag!" A cousin of Melville's had presided at the court martial, and no doubt this fact made the event particularly significant for Melville.[6] For something like three years he worked at what may have been at first a mere sketch in prose, then a short story, and finally a novelette based upon the *Somers* mutiny. Perhaps never actually completed in the form ultimately desired by its author, the story *(Billy Budd, Sailor)*, as left for posterity, was written down in a well-patched, much-revised manuscript by April of 1891.[7]

Excepting for deaths among his family and friends, the closing years of life treated Melville kindly. He had no financial worries; for various bequests by wealthy relatives had made him not only secure but prosperous. He possessed the leisure to do his writing — or neglect it — without external pressures, to savor his garden, and now and then to relax with his grandchildren. In health he was almost vigorous, although a long walk in the cold air one day in January, 1891, brought on a spell of dizziness. He published another volume of poems in a privately printed edition in May, 1891. *Timoleon* contains verses having to do largely with Melville's personal experiences and emotions or with subjects easily traceable to his reading. He was in the process of preparing still another book of poems, *Weeds and Wildings* — this one especially for Lizzie — when his work was interrupted by illness in June. The book was never finished. As his heart weakened, his condition gradually grew worse. On September 28 he died, leaving the manuscript of *Billy Budd* and the poetic fragments behind him in the famous tin box that remained nearly undisturbed for a generation until it was ransacked by Raymond Weaver, first of the modern Melville scholars.

The obituaries in the New York newspapers generally referred to Melville as an author who had once been popular, whose best work was an adventure story of the South Seas called *Typee*, and who at his death was relatively forgotten.

CHAPTER 5

Loomings

I 1he Man Who Lived among the Cannibals

SINCE his youthful "Fragments from a Writing Desk" (1839) must be classified as juvenilia rather than dignified with consideration as true literature, any discussion of Melville's place in the American literary scene necessarily begins with *Typee*. This work first appeared in London on February 27, 1846, when John Murray published it in two parts in his Home and Colonial Library as *Narrative of a Four Months' Residence among the Natives of a Valley of the Marquesas Islands*. Three weeks later, under an American copyright, Wiley and Putnam of New York issued the book in a single volume in the Library of Choice Reading series as *Typee: A Peep at Polynesian Life*. The story was hailed immediately on both sides of the Atlantic with enthusiastic praise; nearly all critics remarked upon its delightful readability.

If there was any fly in the ointment, it consisted of the doubts raised regarding the authenticity of certain details. Murray, who had presented the book to readers as a strictly factual account of life in a primitive society, was inclined momentarily to suspect Melville of a literary fraud. When critics hinted that such fascinating adventures as *Typee* portrayed could not actually have taken place but must be rank fiction, Murray demanded proof that the author had really visited the South Seas. This demand naturally embarrassed Melville, who had improved his tale by deliberately heightening the dramatic tension, lengthening the time sequence, 'and adding various embellishments. He therefore breathed more freely when, during June, Richard Tobias Greene wrote a letter to the *Buffalo Commercial Advertiser*[1] vouching for the work and identifying himself as the companion of Melville's exploits. "I am the true and veritable 'Toby,' yet living," he declared, " and I am happy to testify to the entire accuracy of the work...."² This unexpected succor inspired Melville to write an additional chapter, "The Story of Toby," first released separately and then incorporated in a revised and expurgated edition of the entire book. In the new American edition, Melville, at the insistence of Wiley and Putnam's editor, Evert Duyckinck, eliminated uncomplimentary references to the practices of the South Seas missionaries and a section dealing with the French occupation of Tahiti. English editions, however, remained unexpurgated and simply appended the sequel.

Typee racily depicts the exciting incidents of Melville's desertion with Greene from the whaling ship *Acushnet* (renamed the *Dolly* in his book) at Nuku Hiva in the Marquesas Islands, their accidental blundering into a valley of reputed cannibals, their observations of life among the uncivilized islanders, and the separate escapes of the two men after adventures both warming and chilling to the blood. The literary effectiveness of the story depends mainly upon its exotic Polynesian setting and upon the pervading suspense entailed in its hero's more and more anxious determination to leave the valley before falling victim to the islanders' cannibalism. Even without this mood of suspense, *Typee* would be a remarkably interesting book; the freshness of its descriptions, far more vivid than those of the ordinary book of travel, is apparent now as it must have been to Melville's first readers. And what reader can ever forget the sight of the lovely brown maidens who swim naked across the bay of Nuku Hiva to greet the *Dolly* — or of the mischievous Fayaway holding her single tappa-cloth garment in the wind before her as a sail? Yet without the growing sense of terror that slowly assumes domination of both narrator and reader throughout the latter half of the tale, this charming romance might not have become the literary bombshell and bestseller that it proved in 1846. No other travel book of the time could even faintly compare to it for interest.

Though *Typee* is, as Thorp has noted, more nearly artless than anything else Melville ever composed,³ and though at first he may well have intended nothing more than to present a straightforward account of his experiences in the Marquesas, Melville's innate artistry impelled him to make important alterations in the facts for dramatic effect. These alterations, each improving the narrative, can hardly be attributable to a poor memory. He extended the period of his captivity in the story to four times its true length, from four weeks to four months. (It would be possible to argue, of course, that any time spent among savage cannibals could well have seemed longer than it actually was!) On the other hand, Melville's obvious efforts to achieve a semblance of accuracy in geographical and ethnological detail are indicated by his extensive use of the source books and standard works of South Seas travel available to him, such as the *Polynesian Researches* of William Ellis and Charles S. Stewart's *A Visit to the South Seas*. In consulting aids of this kind, he formed a habit, discussed in chapter 1, that immensely influenced his literary methods during the remainder of his career.

One looks vainly in *Typee* — and the same can be said of *Omoo* — for either the philosophical speculation so characteristic of Melville at his best or the awareness, developed later, of the real spirit of accurate scientific observation. Perhaps a kind of common sense philosophy is not wanting, and certainly both *Typee* and *Omoo* contain a sufficient number of observations of primitive man and his customs to be ethnologically useful as well as highly entertaining.[4] Still, Melville's original comments on what he saw among the savages are not to be mistaken for those of a trained observer. While deriding in these works contemporary travel writers who derived their facts at second hand from disreputable beachcombers and South Seas rovers, he himself cannot be relied on as an ethnologist.[5] His chapter on the zoology of the Marquesas Islands describes only what any casual traveler might see: dogs like hairless rats, an occasional cat, golden lizards, bright-colored but voiceless birds, and a troublesome fly.[6] The true scientific world for Melville in 1846 was as distant as Mars. In spite of its realistic appraisal of such factors in South Seas island life as the building habits and religious customs of the natives, *Typee* must be regarded as overwhelmingly romantic.

II   *The Sequel*

Omoo (meaning "the rover"), which appeared in 1847 as a continuation of the story begun in *Typee*, carries forward the account of Melville's adventures after his escape from the Taipi valley. Though rather harder on the missionaries than its predecessor and lacking some of the novelty and suspense of the earlier book, *Omoo* became at once exceedingly popular. If one may judge by the number of copies of the editions published in the 1840's which are available even today, it must have been during Melville's lifetime the most widely read of all his books.[7]

Beginning with a short introduction that relates the work to the preceding narrative, Melville describes in *Omoo* many of the people and places he saw during the months immediately following his departure from the Marquesas Islands. Apparently drawing upon true incidents, he devotes a third of the book to life aboard the unfortunate *Julia*, where the captain's weakness and the mate's drunken incompetence result in a half-hearted mutiny among the crew. He describes in an unresentful and humorous way the open-air calaboose on the island of Tahiti in which he and other accused mutineers were confined. Melville makes clear in the story that his refusal to work on the *Julia* has been induced by an injury to his leg; therefore his incarceration, however casual and wanting in severity it may have been, seems like rank injustice. Some of the crew members he introduces, however, are hardened cases clearly deserving punishment. His particular companion in captivity he calls Doctor Long Ghost (John B. Troy in real life), a disgraced former surgeon who delights in practical jokes and who frequently takes the lead in troublemaking.

These two, after vain efforts to secure a trial, boldly walk away from their jail one day and set out for a neighboring island. Here they work for a time on a potato farm run by two strange characters, a Yankee and a Cockney; then they return to make a tour of Tahiti and observe the customs of the natives. Their adventures are numerous but filled with more amusement than danger. They find the Tahitians fairly subjugated by the missionaires but secretly fond of their old ways. They witness a supposedly forbidden dance of certain "backsliding girls of Tamai," but they find it less wicked than they had supposed it would be. Their attempts at lovemaking fail to arouse any serious response. They mix into native affairs as much as possible but are uniformly met by the diffidence which the Tahitians, after long experience with white sailors and missionaries, exhibit generally toward most strangers. The book ends with its hero starting out upon another whaling voyage.

Omoo is more confident in style than *Typee*, and it is also imbued with a feeling of relaxed good humor. The author seems to be relishing the memory of carefree days passed with an amusing companion on a pleasant, peaceful island. He can look back upon his adventures with a sense of equanimity because they entailed a minimum of risk, and with self-justified pleasure at their innocent nature. While the first portion of the book deals in a semicomic vein with matters that might have had evil consequences, the latter portion merely relates the interesting details of a boyish ramble in a new and exotic land.

Typee contains a plot held firmly together by suspense and rising to an exciting climax; but *Omoo*, like a picaresque novel, loosely strings together a number of minor incidents. While each incident is interesting in itself, what holds the reader is mainly the youthful exuberance and mischievous humor of the telling. Having a less powerful dramatic form, *Omoo* tends to convey a sense of more exact reality. Presumably Melville made fewer changes for dramatic effect in *Omoo* than he did in *Typee*; indeed, it is quite safe to assume that *Omoo*, far more than any other book Melville wrote, pictures events pretty much as they actually occurred. As in the case of *Typee*, Melville drew upon source books to supplement his own observations of primitive life and thus improved the realism of his descriptions. As a writer, Melville displays in *Omoo* a growing confidence and skill in technique — a clear indication that in his first year of authorship he was making lengthy strides toward the mastery of his art.

Melville's third novel, *Mardi*, must have been started while he still was at work on *Omoo*, or not very long afterward. Though it bears the signs of having been planned as a sequel to the two books preceding it and opens with an exhilarating account of life at sea aboard another whaling ship (presumably the *Charles and Henry*), this work differs markedly from *Typee* and *Omoo*; and its characteristics are discussed in chapter 6, along with those of *Moby-Dick* and *Pierre*. As has already been noted, readers of *Mardi*, expecting another *Omoo*, were bitterly shocked at finding it an allegory.

III   *Potboilers*

Surprised by the reaction of his readers to *Mardi*, Melville immediately saw that he must compromise artistic and philosophical principles if he were to hold his audience and to sell his books. The results of this compromise were the novels *Redburn* (1849) and *White-Jacket* (1850). The action of *Redburn*, originally entitled in manuscript *My First Voyage*, is based upon Melville's experiences in 1839 as a "boy" aboard the packet *St. Lawrence*.

Like Richard Henry Dana's *Two Years before the Mast*, which *Redburn* resembles in a number of ways, this book is less a story of maritime adventure than a semifictional account of nautical reminiscence. It was long accepted as a kind of personal journal of the voyage, but William Gilman's careful study of its origins has proved it to be beyond question a skillful blend of artful fiction and remembered fact.[8] Since the trip to Liverpool and back to New York provided somewhat bare materials for a novel, especially when the theme of first voyages by sons-of-gentlemen had by this time been pretty thoroughly played out by the British writers, Melville necessarily turned for ideas both to his imagination and to source books. For some of his details he borrowed freely from such works as Captain Marryat's *Peter Simple* and the anonymous *Picture of Liverpool* (1808).

When referring to *Redburn* in private, Melville characterized it with a show of contempt as "beggarly"[9] and as written "almost entirely for 'lucre' — by the job, as a wood-sawyer saws wood...."[10] Yet the book has attracted and held the rapt attention of many intelligent and discriminating readers; and, as Gilman shows, in complexity of style and thought it ranks on a distinctly higher plane than either *Typee* or *Omoo*.

Redburn's principal theme is the discovery of life's crude realities by a young idealist of puritanical tendencies. Pampered in boyhood and reared in almost complete ignorance of the world's frightening brutality and social evils, Wellingborough Redburn, the hero, confronts the rigors of back-breaking toil, filth, official tyranny, and the enforced companionship of depraved sailors on board the *Highlander* — not to mention the twin horrors of disease and starving poverty in the Liverpool slums. In his innocence he accepts the friendship of a spoiled and rather sophisticated youth who is later seen as an inveterate gambler, egotistical dandy, and victim of stupid social ambitions.

Characters in *Redburn* are developed more fully and appear substantially more like real people than those in the earlier works. The pathetic Harry Bolton, a lost soul in the maelstrom of life, reveals before his tragic end contradictions of character that make him far more interesting than the uncomplicated Long Ghost. The unregenerate Jackson, a sailor who dies horribly in a fall from the yardarm, is the first of several persons in Melville's books who embody the principle of absolute evil.

The book betrays Melville's growing concern for social reform and his recognition of the alarming disparity between man's professions of belief and his true attitudes. Redburn observes the callous treatment of the poor and unfortunate by the Christian people of Liverpool and by such arrant rascals as the captain of the *Highlander*, who regards the helpless as his just prey. During his voyage the fledgling sailor, though courteous and kindhearted, is treated with rude contempt by his fellow crew members, nearly all his intellectual and social inferiors; and, at the close of his voyage, he is outrageously cheated of his wages.

A study in youthful disillusionment, the book recounts a whole catalog of disappointments and frustrations; for the hero, the main ones are his failures to find a hotel once visited by his father, to realize his cherished hope of seeing the glories of London, and to receive his pay after a hard voyage. In spite of its theme of disillusionment and social criticism, however, this cannot be called a bitter novel; on the contrary, *Redburn* is written in a good-humored vein — a mood in which the disappointment of young idealism is accepted as a natural and rather amusing part of life.

IV   *Man-Of-War*

White-Jacket (1850), subtitled "The World in a Man-of-War," contains examples of some of Melville's best writing; and it would be a great book were it not that it lacks a dramatic theme and a protagonist of mighty stature. In contrast to this earlier novel, *Moby-Dick* (1851) is tightly unified by the far-ranging hunt for the White Whale and by its elaborate but meaningful philosophical symbolism; in addition, it has for its hero one of the most powerful single figures in literature. *White-Jacket*, though an extremely fine book, never quite reaches the heights; for, like *Redburn*, it was written in a hurry and was always considered by its author to be nothing more than a potboiler.

The story roughly follows the course of Melville's voyage from Honolulu to Boston as a common sailor aboard the *United States* in 1843-1844. To the incidents of the voyage Melville added some comments and episodes from his own imagination and also a large body of interesting material taken from James Mercier's *Life in a Man-of-War* and from such popular sea tales as Tobias Smollett's *Roderick Random* and Nathaniel Ames' *A Mariner's Sketches*. The borrowed portions, under Melville's now-practiced hand, breathe and pulse with life so vivid that for years Melville scholars stubbornly resisted the idea that such thrilling scenes as the hero's fall from the mast into the wild ocean were not records of his own direct experience. Eventually a search of the man-of-war's logbook proved that some of the incidents described in the book had never occurred, and their sources were traced easily to Melville's reading. Yet their power to persuade belief remains; it is the truth of art, not the truth of actual experience, that gives these moving incidents their verisimilitude.

As might be expected, the leading characters in *White-Jacket*, though presented for the most part under fictitious names and with various alterations for dramatic effect, are drawn very largely from life — a fairly common practice, as has already been noted, in Melville's writing. In *White-Jacket*, some of whose characters are officers in the United States Navy, Melville intentionally disguised several of the persons he described (especially those with reprehensible habits), or he combined the traits of two or more persons into one. He may have recalled that, after the publication of *Omoo*, a number of the persons portrayed in that book (notably Dr. Johnstone) had been offended at being too easily recognized by visitors to Tahiti. The most admirable of all the characters in *White-Jacket* is Jack Chase (previously mentioned in chapter 2), captain of the foretop and a well-read, courageous, and eminently noble figure who made a lifelong impression on Melville. Others include Captain Claret, a capable officer unfortunately addicted to drink; the clever but wicked master-at-arms Bland, who foreshadows the monstrous Claggart in Melville's *Billy Budd*; and the narrator, White-Jacket himself, inventor of the multilayered coat, sewn from innumerable scraps of cloth, that gave him his name.

The book as a whole effectively describes the life of a sailor on an American warship of the nineteenth century. It consists in a series of absorbingly interesting sketches and episodes unified chiefly by the fact that they take place consecutively on board a single ship with one cast of characters. Like the *Pequod* in *Moby-Dick* and the *Fidèle* in *The Confidence-Man,* the frigate *Neversink* is the world in microcosm. Melville finds it a world organized wholly upon military principles; and every institution in it, including the church of the peacemaker Christ, is adapted ingeniously to the uses of war. A chaplain plays an important role in all formal ceremonies and sanctions by his presence and prayers the "obsolete barbarism" of the savage system; he even shares in the bounty payable under the Articles of War when an American fighting ship sinks an enemy, "destroying ships full of human beings." Thus, in the man-of-war world, the church condones murder for profit. In general, the effect of the system he describes is, to Melville, destructive of individual worth and morally degrading,'' emphatically a system of cruel cogs and wheels, systematically grinding up in one common hopper all that might minister to the moral well-being of the crew.''

Among all the evils that Melville found rampant on the *Neversink*, one of those most colorfully set forth and most heartily condemned is the custom of merciless flogging for minor offenses. Even under a representative government established solely for the purpose of protecting the rights of citizens, he implies, the individual can be legally chastised and humiliated as if he possessed no rights at all. Editorializing, he joins his voice to those of many others who in 1850 were condemning the practice:

Irrespective of incidental considerations, we assert that flogging in the navy is opposed to the essential dignity of man, which no legislator has a right to violate; that it is oppressive, and glaringly unequal in its operations; that it is utterly repugnant to the spirit of our democratic institutions; indeed that it involves a lingering trait of the worst times of a barbarous feudal aristocracy: in a word, we denounce it as religiously, morally, and immutably *wrong*. (chap. 35)

The fact that the crew may contain ''scores of desperadoes'' does not justify flogging; for, says Melville, ''[d]epravity in the oppressed is no apology for the oppressor.''

Some of the supposed evils presented in the book, however, must have been fancied rather than real. His infamous Dr. Cuticle, for example, would hardly have been permitted on an American ship of the nineteenth century to perform his feats of surgery in the heartless and bloody manner Melville pretends to have witnessed; Cuticle obviously is the fictional counterpart of the fascinatingly repulsive Dr. Mackshane in *Roderick Random*. One may see in Cuticle, with his grand collection of morbid medical specimens, the representative of science; and Melville's treatment of him is typical for the nineteenth-century romanticist. One of the common complaints of the romanticist against science — time and again expounded by such poets as Wordsworth — is that science in its cold quest for facts tends to destroy beauty and to ignore human feeling. Though he was later to be drawn more and more inexorably toward an attitude of scientific realism, Melville never entirely lost his antagonism toward the Cuticles and Margoths of the world.

Beautifully written, with language verging on the poetic — ''a soft, seething, foamy lull''; ''the speechless profound of the sea'';

"shrouded masts . . . like the apparitions of three gigantic Turkish Emirs striding over the ocean"; "the books that prove most agreeable, grateful, and companionable, are those we pick up by chance here and there; those which seem put into our hands by Providence; those which pretend to little, but abound in much" — *White-Jacket,* with all its humorous and serious comments on the good and evil of any man-of-war world, is so nearly a great book that the reader cannot help wishing, as Hawthorne did for *Mardi,*[11] that its author had spent more pains to make it even better.

In the final chapter the symbolism of the tale is made specific:

> As a man-of-war that sails through the sea, so this earth that sails through the air. We mortals are all on board as fast-sailing, never-sinking, world-frigate, of which God was the shipwright; and she is but one craft in a Milky-Way fleet, of which God is the Lord High Admiral. The port we sail from is forever astern. And though far out of sight of land, for ages and ages we continue to sail with sealed orders, and our last destination remains a secret to ourselves and our officers; yet our final haven was predestinated ere we slipped from the stocks at Creation.
>
> Thus sailing with sealed orders, we ourselves are the repositories of the secret packet, whose mysterious contents we long to learn. There are no mysteries out of ourselves.
>
> Oh, shipmates and world-mates, all round! we the people suffer many abuses. Our gun-deck is full of complaints. In vain from Lieutenants do we appeal to the Captain; in vain—while on board our world-frigate—to the indefinite Navy Commissioners, so far out of sight aloft. Yet the worst of our evils we blindly inflict upon ourselves; our officers cannot remove them, even if they would. From the last ills no being can save another; therein each man must be his own saviour. For the rest, whatever befall us, let us never train our murderous guns inboard; let us not mutiny with bloody pikes in our hands.

Throughout the reading of *White-Jacket,* one is aware of a sense of restraint; because of his bad luck with *Mardi,* Melville did not release in *White-Jacket* the full power of his desire to philosophize. The social and political criticism is presented in a relatively objective spirit, without the usual passion of the crusading reformer. Nevertheless, the book as a whole constitutes a damaging commentary on life as Melville saw it and a plea for brotherly efforts "to civilize civilization and christianize Christendom."

CHAPTER 6

The Everlasting No

I Chartless Voyage

IN *MARDI, Moby-Dick,* and *Pierre,* Melville presents three aspects of man's intellectual and spiritual existence—man as "the fool of Truth, the fool of Fate, and the fool of Virtue." Together these novels reveal nearly every major facet of Melville's philosophical speculation during the most important period of his literary career.

Mardi was the first of Melville's works to contain, as he confided frankly to Hawthorne, "what I feel most moved to write."[1] Though it opens as a breath-takingly exciting sea story, striking the reader at once as an improvement upon *Typee* and *Omoo,* it changes almost abruptly after several intriguing chapters to something vastly different. This change, as noted earlier, shocked and repelled Melville's nineteenth-century readers. The early chapters, in which the narrator and an old sailor companion ingeniously desert their ship in mid-ocean and sail for many days in a small boat seeking land, sparkle with lively details and mounting suspense and thus lead the reader to classify the book as one of the most thrilling of maritime adventure novels. Reading further in the grip of the fascinating narrative and confidently expecting more of this type of entertainment, the reader suddenly and perhaps unbelievingly finds himself—not long after the hero-narrator lands on an island, where he is given the name of Taji—in the midst of a surprising allegory peopled with characters who are personifications rather than real persons.

Among the most prominent of these characters are King Media, representing the mind; Mohi, history; Babbalanja, philosophy; Yoomy, poetry; and so on.[2] Taji clearly represents the human soul, or Melville himself. Philosophers, writers, historical personages, and nations are mentioned in the story under fictitious names. The United States, for example, is described in the section on Vivenza; and Great Britain is called (appropriately, for that era) Dominora. Dante is introduced under the name of Lombardo, and *The Divine Comedy* is referred to as Kostanza. There are also in the book two glamorous but patently unreal women characters, the temptress Hautia, who seems to stand for wordliness and sensuality, and the beautiful Yillah, with whom Taji falls in love. The search for Yillah, who disappears very shortly after the hero has begun to appreciate her loveliness, forms the main basis for the allegory. To Melville she means the ultimate revelation—the secret of the universe.

As the allegorical portion of *Mardi* (about three-quarters of the entire book) begins, Taji has the good fortune to rescue Yillah from a savage priest and his three sons (often interpreted as a reference to the Trinity), who are conducting her to the sacrifice. Remaining only long enough to arouse in Taji the most fiery desires, Yillah mysteriously disappears, taking from Taji the ethereal Eden which he has barely glimpsed. On the advice of his friends, chief among whom is Media (mind), the frantic Taji sets out upon a journey through the world in quest of his lost love. This is as much as to say that the philosophical seeker (in the finest romantic tradition), having once tasted the joys of discovering Truth, but strangely losing sight of it, now launches himself upon an urgent but studious pursuit in order to recapture its beauty and thereby to restore his peace of mind.

On his search Taji is accompanied by Media, Mohi, Babbalanja, and Yoomy; and he is relentlessly pursued by tradition and conscience in the shape of the three sons of the priest he has murdered (supposedly representing the religious faith of his youth). The searchers go from country to country through an imaginary archipelago of the South Pacific. Everywhere inquiring for his lost Yillah, Taji and his friends allegorically subject these mythical countries to an elaborate philosophical scrutiny. But the object of their search, in spite of the occasional traces they find of her, always eludes them. Truth, with its promise of beauty and final happiness, is nowhere to be found.

In the course of the allegory Melville examines the customs and manners of mankind, religion, philosophical systems, literature, government, ethics, and the human ego. The comments of the judicious Media, the talkative Babbalanja, the pompous Mohi, and the fanciful Yoomy, as well as the observations of Taji himself, serve to display Melville's keen interest in all these matters and his youthful idealism in the search for truth. They also reveal a richness of imagination and an enthusiasm for philosophical inquiry hardly to be suspected in the author of *Typee* and *Omoo*. Even the most cursory interpretation of the allegory shows Melville's familiarity with the great philosophers and writers. He refers to Dante with tremendous respect and affection. He examines historical events with a keen eye, expressing equal disapproval of the British empire-building and of the mob psychology of Jacksonian democracy. He throws in comments against slavery, and he questions a system of elections in which candidates and issues are at the mercy of mere popular whim. He condemns as fraudulent the claims of dogmatic church organizations to the exclusive ownership of true doctrine or of divinely granted power over the souls of men. He finds war inglorious and largely degrading. At the same time, he shows his delight in human companionship, in the sharing of dangers, pleasures, and ideas. His characters carry on much brilliant conversation; they argue, sing, drink, and playfully disport themselves.

All the searchers in the party, excepting Taji, finally give up the pursuit and find safe harbor at Serenia, the island of Christian love (or primitive Christianity), whose inhabitants have set aside their desire to know the secrets of God and are satisfied to live together peacefully under the Golden Rule. They recognize human weakness and cheerfully accept it as their common lot. Acknowledging the fact of man's inability to discover the Absolute, they believe that greater good for mankind lies in achieving a neighborly way of life. To Taji alone, who insists on storming heaven for Truth, although he suspects that the secrets he may learn there are not really worth all his trouble,[3] Serenia offers no contentment. He continues his quest, finding an "almost-Yillah" in the enjoyment of purely material pleasures under the guidance of Hautia, but at the sacrifice of spiritual innocence. In the end, having sought throughout the entire world in vain, he deliberately and as an act of supreme self-assertion takes his own life in order to pursue the search for his Yillah into the "outer ocean" of the afterworld.

Why Melville should have written a book in two distinct styles, composed of two sets of actions—one highly realistic and the other allegorical—only incidentally related to each other, with different casts of characters for the two parts, has puzzled his readers for generations. Many explain it by supposing—and the evidence is fairly convincing—that he started *Mardi* as a sequel to *Omoo,* intending to base it upon the events of his third whaling voyage but that, running out of good material for the story, he was encouraged by his yarn-spinning propensities to abandon real for imaginative incidents.[4] The romantically colorful narrative of the allegorical portion may have been suggested by some of the popular German romances of that era, crammed with warm excitement, impossible wonders, and mysterious feminine wiles—for example, such a book as La Motte-Fouqué's *Undine.*[5] Leon Howard has hypothesized that much of *Mardi* was written to interest women and that it was composed under the personal influence of Elizabeth, Melville's young bride, who deeply loved romantic novels and had a special fondness for the involved flower symbolism that appears throughout the work.[6] Whatever other factors may have influenced him in the composition of *Mardi,* Melville's voluminous reading undoubtedly determined the ultimate form and content of the book. No one who reads it can avoid being reminded constantly of Spenser's *Faerie Queene,* Dante's *Divine Comedy,* and Burton's *Anatomy of Melancholy*—not to mention Rabelais and Sir Thomas Browne.

Once having launched his hero on the worldwide search for his ideal, Melville seems to have allowed his mind free play to wander in every direction that attracted him. The device of a prolonged exploration under the guidance of intellect, philosophy, history, and literature he probably borrowed from Dante. Other symbolism and the rich imagery of certain scenes were no doubt inspired by Spenser; Hautia, for instance, reminds us of Spenser's false but alluring Duessa, her abode a delusive Bower of Bliss. The language of Rabelais breaks through in scenes of rollicking revelry and in incident after incident of hilarious fun cloaking the most serious and biting social satire. From reading the great writers of allegory, rather than from the analysis of his own experience or formal studies of academic subject matter, Melville developed and used his interest in moral, social, and political philosophy.

The device of an allegorical voyage is a fairly common one in literature. Books 4 and 5 of Rabelais' *Gargantua and Pantagruel,* a work highly admired by American intellectuals at Melville's time, describe a voyage by the giant Pantagruel and a group of talkative companions to numerous fictitious islands. This provided an easy pattern for *Mardi* to copy. In his preface to the fourth book of his translation of Rabelais, Peter Motteux gives this description:

[A]s Homer in his *Odysses* maked his Hero wander Ten Years through most parts of the then known World, so Rabelais, in a Three-months Voyage makes Pantagruel take a View of almost all sorts of People and Professions: with this difference however between the Ancient Mythologist and the Modern, That while the *Odysses* has been compar'd to a setting Sun, in respect to the *Iliads,* Rabelais' last Work, which is this Voyage to the *Oracle of the Bottle,* (by which he means Truth) is justly thought his Masterpiece; being writ with more Spirit, Salt, and Flame, than the First Part of his Works.

Mardi, however, suffers not only from the sudden change that occurred in its author's original plan of composition but also from being a rather loosely constructed allegory rather than one which is tightly knit and unified by elimination of extraneous matter. The story wanders into a multitude of byways not on the main path of the allegorical action and attempts to criticize too many aspects of life all at once. Melville himself recognized this failing and confessed it in the book when he remarked, "I have chartless voyaged."

Nevertheless, because of its resemblance to the German romance, its rich imagery, its high good humor, and its adventure, Melville believed *Mardi* to be not only a better book than either *Typee* or *Omoo* but better calculated for popularity. Confidently expecting to hear little but plaudits from the critics, he made a particular point of calling attention in his preface to the difference between this work and its two predecessors. Half-jokingly, but certainly with no intention to mislead,[7] he informed his prospective readers by way of explanation: "Having published two narratives of voyages in the Pacific, which, in many quarters, were received with incredulity, the thought occurred to me of indeed writing a romance of Polynesian adventure, and publishing it as such; to see whether the fiction might not, possibly, be received for a verity: in some degree the reverse of my previous experience."

This ought to have been a fair enough warning, besides constituting a sly dig at the critics who had censured the earlier books for alleged embellishment of the truth; but readers immediately resented what they considered an imposture. Not that they did not welcome entertainment. In a book about the exotic South Seas, however, they apparently expected fancy to be heavily coated with fact, rather than vice versa. Some readers openly questioned the mental balance of an author who could mix philosophical, religious, literary, and political speculation into a tale presented as romance. In reading a romance, presumably, the reader should not be required to think.

A factual narrative might have been accepted, even with some embellishments, after the delightful examples of *Typee* and *Omoo*. A pure romance in the German style might well have enlarged the circle of Melville's readers and perhaps raised admiration for the author's versatility. Mixing the two styles and adding the foreign element of thoughtful allegory, on the other hand, resulted in little but confusion. Instead of the bestseller he had envisioned, Melville had a book for which he began to spend much of his time apologizing.[8] The outcome served not only as a blow to Melville's literary ambition, demonstrating his utter naiveté in the profession of authorship, but also as a lesson that he never forgot. Painful as the lesson was, it forced him eventually to the discovery of a masterly technique for clothing his most significant ideas in a more interesting and palatable form in *Moby-Dick*.

II *Saga of the White Whale*

If there proved to be too much outright allegory in *Mardi*, the offense to American literary taste was conscientiously corrected in *Moby-Dick*. Both books deal, however, with essentially the same philosophical problem: the search for a true explanation of man's relationship to God in the universe. In that sense an allegory is present in *Moby-Dick* as well as in *Mardi;* but, by discovering a new method of writing, Melville was able to conceal it so thoroughly that some readers are not even aware of its presence. For the change in his method Melville could credit not only the scars left by *Mardi's* unfavorable reception but also certain techniques learned from reading Thomas Carlyle's brilliant philosophical essay, *Sartor Resartus*. As already noted in chapter 3, Melville read this remarkable work just as he was beginning the story of the White Whale.[9]

As in the case of *Mardi,* Melville produced in *Moby-Dick* a novel vastly different from the straightforward narrative that he apparently first intended. His comments describing the book to Richard Bentley, the London publisher, in 1850 show unmistakably that his purpose at the beginning was to write a more or less factual account of whales and whaling embroidered with incidents and legends of the southern fisheries.[10] Having just gone through the admittedly uninspiring experience of dashing off *Redburn* and *White-Jacket,* both of which he classified in his own estimation as pure hackwork, he seems to have been looking, consciously or unconsciously, for some acceptable device to combine in one book a marketable narrative of adventure and the kind of moral and philosophical speculation in which he had allowed himself to become deeply involved. He knew that, in order to sell, his book must be entertaining; yet his persistent inner desires impelled him to reveal his deeper thoughts.

The way to bring this about he discovered in Carlyle. Though many readers of the nineteenth century missed the real point of Carlyle's emotional self-analysis in *Sartor Resartus,* readers of today, understanding more of psychology, readily grasp its powerful revelations. In the pretended biography of Professor Diogenes Teufelsdröckh and the translation of his treatise on clothes is concealed Carlyle's moving spiritual autobiography and a firm statement of his moral philosophy. The method employed—that of clothing the profoundest abstract ideas in the trappings of symbol and holding the reader's rapt attention by means of skillful humor and concrete incident—must have impressed Melville as favorably as did Carlyle's forward-looking ideas.

In Carlyle he found an emergent sense of scientific realism to which his own mind, prepared by his previous reading and his experience, quickly responded. Carlyle, for example, did not regard nature as Wordsworth and the other great romanticists regarded it—as a bland, beautiful, and beneficent influence—but more nearly in the Darwinian view as cruel and murderous beneath its outward finery. Though perhaps not entirely aware of it, Carlyle had already partially adopted the attitudes of the coming age of science. He was not completely happy in exchanging a comfortable romanticism for a more barren realism; but, like the scientists of his day, he was beginning to see the inadequacy of the romantic vision of things. In *Past and Present* (1843), which Melville probably read, Carlyle spoke frankly of the natural world as "a thing of teeth and claws; Nature is a dumb lioness, deaf to thy pleadings, fiercely devouring." This bears a striking resemblance to the language used in *Moby-Dick,* where Melville makes numerous references to the savage cruelty "treacherously hidden beneath the loveliest tints of azure" in wild nature and to "the universal cannibalism of the sea; all whose creatures prey upon each other, carrying on eternal war since the world began.''

Both Carlyle and Melville display clearly an antiromantic point of view; but neither can be considered a confirmed realist or, for that matter, a Darwinian. The time for this eventuality was not quite ripe. Scientific realism, nevertheless, laid its finger on both and stirred them to the depths. What Melville found most admirable in Carlyle, one may infer, was his intellectual honesty. To Carlyle, student of Kantian philosophy and transcendentalism, true reality lay hidden under the cloak of perceived facts (the symbols or ''clothing'' of nature)—a concept of startling significance for Melville, who made use of it in what has come to be perhaps the most familiar passage in *Moby-Dick*. In a tense and vital speech Captain Ahab tries to describe for the benefit of Starbuck, his first mate, the real reasons for his mad hunt of the White Whale. How much this explanation depends upon Carlyle may be seen in the following quotation from *Sartor Resartus* relating to the nature of reality:

> All visible things are emblems; what thou seest is not there on its own account; strictly taken, is not there at all: Matter exists only spiritually, and to represent some Idea, and *body* it forth. . . . On the other hand, all Emblematic things are properly Clothes, thought-woven or hand-woven: must not the Imagination weave Garments, visible Bodies, wherein the else invisible creations and inspirations of our Reason are, like Spirits, revealed, and first become all-powerful. . . ?[11]

Accepting this view of reality, Melville declares through Ahab his intention of reaching truth by striking through the mask of matter, the mere emblem of reality, to the spirit behind it, the faint moldings of whose features he dimly discerns. Ahab is, therefore, repeating Carlyle when he explains the nature of the universe to Starbuck:

> All visible objects, man, are but as pasteboard masks. But in each event—in the living act, the undoubted deed—there, some unknown but still reasoning thing puts forth the mouldings of its features from behind the unreasoning mask. If man will strike, strike through the mask!

And he adds:

> Talk not to me of blasphemy, man; I'd strike the sun if it insulted me. For could the sun do that, then could I do the other: since there is ever a sort of

fair play herein, jealousy presiding over all creations. But not my master, man, is even that fair play. Who's over me? Truth hath no confines.

Close examination of *Sartor Resartus* will uncover additional evidence of Melville's use of Carlyle in writing *Moby-Dick*. One minor example may be found in Carlyle's reference to his hero as an "Ishmael." Teufelsdröckh at the university meets with little but ignorance and indifference, and thus, remarks Carlyle, "in the destitution of the wild desert does our young Ishmael acquire for himself the highest of all possessions, that of Self-help." Even the language of *Moby-Dick* reflects Carlyle. It is manly and powerful rather than liquidly flowing; it is full of inversions, elaborately wrought sentences, and explosive emphasis. Melville's use of "thee" and "thou" may well have been dictated by the example of Carlyle (certainly not by the fact that some of his characters are Quakers!) although there is a long tradition of "thee" and "thou" in English romantic literature, and even Hawthorne followed the custom.

The plot of *Moby-Dick,* in simplest outline, depicts the hunt for a white whale by a sea captain from Nantucket. The captain, intellectually brilliant and spiritually courageous but also clearly insane, has lost a leg, bitten off during a previous whaling cruise by Moby Dick, the whale. Refusing to suffer this misfortune quietly as one of the common hazards of his trade, Ahab regards it instead as an instance of supernatural malice and vows revenge. He directs the crew of the *Pequod* (a world in miniature) in a persistent and cunning search for Moby Dick throughout the whaling grounds of the Pacific; he enlists the men's support by offering to reward the one who first sights the whale, and he instills in them some of his own hatred for the creature that has maimed him. Only Starbuck, his efficient and sensible fellow officer, attempts to dissuade Ahab from the chase. For his own purposes Ahab carries on board as his personal boat crew a mysterious group of Parsees, the leader of whom, Fedallah, is a fortune-teller. After weeks of search, Moby Dick is finally sighted and attacked. Endowed with a strength and savagery far beyond the skill of his pursuers, he not only destroys Ahab and Fedallah but sinks the ship by ramming it. The main events of the story are told by a young sailor named Ishmael, who has joined the crew of the *Pequod* for his first whaling voyage and who survives the wreck by clinging to a coffin. Ishmael describes not only Ahab's tragic adventure but many other matters that interest him as a newcomer to whaling: the ship, the crew, the whaling industry, the various kinds of whale, the sea, and his own thoughts.

By introducing so many subjects only incidentally related to the main plot, Melville made *Moby-Dick* a novel that fits no ready classification. The book is far more than the racy story of maritime adventure, representing the American spirit of restlessness, that Richardson made it out to be in his nineteenth-century history and appraisal of American literature.[12] It is, first of all, a fairly reliable treatise on whales and whaling. The cetological materials in *Moby-Dick* reveal a thorough knowledge of this field. They are incomparably better handled and more scientifically accurate than the plentiful zoological information that Melville scattered through *Mardi* (which contains, among other things, a pseudoscientific chapter on sharks). In the years between the two books Melville read much on science and consequently became far more discriminating in the selection and use of scientific sourcebooks. The fact that Melville included so vast a quantity of cetology in his novel has, of course, puzzled many readers. The idea of doing so may have been suggested by Richard Henry Dana. Such information would naturally have proved interesting to an apprentice whaler like Ishmael. Furthermore, in the presentation of the cetological matter there is mixed a great deal of Melville's characteristic humor. Nevertheless, for some readers its inclusion constitutes a serious defect in the book. Others regard the cetological material as the remnant of Melville's original plan; beginning the book as a factual account of whales and whaling, they believe, he became dissatisfied with his product and rewrote it as a symbolical novel.[13] Artistically considered, the sections on cetology add a sense of realism to the story: they contribute character and individuality to one of the principal actors in the drama, the White Whale himself.

Secondly, the nature of the plot and the dramatic form into which it is cast provide numerous opportunities for Melville to insert at frequent intervals his comments, either as dramatic asides or as digressions, upon the universe and human destiny. These comments are often placed in the mouth of Ishmael as narrator, but they are spoken under a variety of circumstances by several other characters as well. One of the problems in reading *Moby-Dick* is to remember when Ishmael speaks as Ishmael the young sailor and when he really speaks as alter ego for the author.[14]

Gradually, but more and more as the story progresses, Melville adopts the course taken by Cyrano de Bergerac when the latter was wooing Roxane through the medium of her lover, Christian. "This grows too difficult," he seems to murmur at last; whereupon, pushing the less articulate Ishmael aside, he proceeds to speak in his own voice.

Thirdly, *Moby-Dick* is a novel thickly strewn with symbolism of many kinds. Under an outward layer of narrative Melville conceals deep philosophical speculation about God and nature. This, after all, is one of the factors that makes the story important; for admittedly the mere tale of mad Ahab's pursuit of a whale, however exciting in itself, offers too thin a foundation for true literary greatness. Why, after all, should a man of Ahab's brilliant natural endowments be found willing to waste his time and effort, losing both ship and life in the process, for a rather pointless vengeance upon a wild whale—a thoughtless brute of the sea? Except as an unusual case study in abnormal psychology, the whole adventure lacks good sense and conviction. If revenge upon the whale were the sole reason for his voyage, Ahab would not be the hero that he is but only a madman of little consequence to literature. Readers of the nineteenth century, to be sure, were familiar with a whole galaxy of noble-souled, romantic heroes who performed senseless and invariably dangerous feats for no reason other than the satisfaction of powerful inner urges. Such heroes, however, generally fail to sustain the interest of readers in the twentieth century. They have no convincing motives for their deeds. Ahab clearly does; and his motives consist of more than the simple joys of the hunter or a spiteful revenge upon an unthinking animal.

III   *Symbols*

What were Ahab's true motives for the pursuit of Moby Dick? This is the key that unlocks the main mystery. Failure to answer this question correctly means misunderstanding the theme of Melville's masterpiece. Attempts to interpret *Moby-Dick* as a carefully constructed allegory have resulted in the proposal of different answers by different critics, but, in the long run, they have proved mainly how difficult has been the task of reading Melville's intentions through his profusion of symbols. Obviously, all the proposed interpretations cannot be right. How, then, can the reader determine which one is correct—which answer Melville himself would have given to the question of Ahab's motives?

Fortunately, Melville has provided clear guidelines in the story, though some critics have displayed a tendency to ignore them. Tempted by the rampant symbolism in the book to indulge themselves in a free play of the imagination, readers have been able to invent various interesting and sometimes elaborate allegorical interpretations, internally consistent, that fit the story fairly well.[15] Almost any reader can find an interpretation that suits his own line of thinking. It is possible, for example, to argue, on the basis of a Freudian psychology, that the White Whale represents Melville's Puritan conscience, against which his ego is engaged in a life-or-death struggle. Others may prefer the theory that the whale stands for evil and Ahab for a modern Christ or Prometheus resisting its power. Still others equate the whale with religion and Ahab with liberal thinking. The contest may even suggest a struggle between individualism and social convention, or between Marxism and capitalism, or between science and nature, or any one of a dozen plausible combinations, none of which Melville had in mind. A case can be made for almost any set of ideas which the reader sees to be in conflict in human life; and apparently, once a person has convinced himself that his particular interpretation of the story is possible, no one can dissuade him from believing it to be the only right one.

But Melville makes no insuperable mystery of the matter. If he had, the book would certainly have to be considered an intellectual failure. Not only does Ahab recognize his own motives (as well as his madness), but he clearly states them. Ahab is—as Melville once admiringly described his friend Hawthorne—"a man who, like Russia or the British Empire, declares himself a sovereign nature (in himself) amid the powers of heaven, hell, and earth. He may perish; but so long as he exists he insists upon treating with all Powers upon an equal basis. If any of those other Powers choose to withhold certain secrets, let them; that does not impair my sovereignty in myself; that does not make me tributary. And perhaps, after all, there is *no* secret."[16] Ahab, too, declares his individual sovereignty, and in doing so he commits the unpardonable sin of thinking himself superior to the rest of mankind. He "would be," says Starbuck, "a democrat to all above; [but] look, how he lords it over all below."

What Ahab seeks—if the reader takes him at his word—is not the actual whale but a symbolical whale—the ultimate mystery of the universe. Being highly educated and a Kantian as well, Ahab acknowledges the limitation of man's power to know God through his intellect; yet, instead of submitting to his weakness, he hopes to transcend it by sheer defiance. His relentless determination to pierce the mystery is precisely that of Taji in *Mardi*. To do so, he believes that he must somehow strike through the "pasteboard mask" of nature; he must reason beyond the emblems of reality. But his puny powers, when matched against the forces of nature and fate, inevitably entrap him. "The painfullest feeling," writes Teufels-drockh, "is that of your own Feebleness *(Unkraft);* ever, as the English Milton says, to be weak is the true misery."[17]

Ahab, although boldly announcing himself a sovereign individual in the spiritual sense, equal in importance if not in strength of mind and body to any other sovereign individual in the universe—"I would strike the sun if he offended me"—is, however, the prisoner of his human form and human limitations. His mind fails in its attempts to pierce the wall of symbol, and his response to the failure is anger both at fate and at his own weakness. He strikes back blindly, even when aware of his doom. For "[h]ow can the prisoner reach outside except by thrusting through the wall?" Braving destruction, he is driven by the desperate urge to know into open defiance of the Power that bound him into weakness and the Mind that remains forever hidden behind the emblematic mask. "Sometimes," he comments bitterly, "I think there's naught beyond." And here he reiterates Melville's own blasphemy: "And perhaps, after all, there is *no* secret."

To argue from this that Melville denied the existence of God or that he regarded God as an enemy is going further than the evidence warrants.[18] While raising serious questions about the inscrutable ways of God and the frustrating mystery of man's place in the universe, Melville took pains to reveal the futility of Ahab's posture of defiance. The appealing thing about Ahab is his courage—though perhaps *foolhardiness* would be a more accurate word—in playing for high stakes with a stacked deck. In his courage to disobey he resembles Prometheus, but there the resemblance ends. In no true sense can he be said to speak or act consistently for Melville, and his example is not recommended for imitation. Again and again in the story the reader is reminded of Ahab's utter madness—the "madness of strength." There is another madman, but quite a different one, in the book. Pip, the

pathetic little Negro boy driven insane after being heartlessly
abandoned for a time on the open ocean, possesses the "madness
of weakness." He never bewails or defies his fate. Yet he, not
Ahab, glimpses in a sudden flash, at the instant of losing sanity, the
true nature of the universe. Melville certainly means to convey in
Moby-Dick the conviction—forced upon him by his own
philosophical inquiries—that, on the one hand, pursuit of the
Absolute leads to frustration and madness; on the other, arrogance
in the search is inherently self-destructive.

Ahab's great error, like Taji's, is failure to accept human
limitations. In assuming the possibility of learning final truth, he
puts himself in effect on a plane of equality with God. Thus he is
not only unrealistic but guilty of the fatal sin of pride; for, like
Ethan Brand in Hawthorne's tale, he believes himself above and
apart from other men. This attitude, though heroic, Melville
plainly condemns. While the climax of *Moby-Dick* seems to come
at the moment when Ahab steps into the whaleboat for the final
confrontation of his nemesis, it really occurs earlier, in the chapter
entitled "The Symphony." In that chapter Ahab for a time
recovers his humanity; he nearly allows himself to be persuaded by
the sympathetic Starbuck to relinquish his vengeful pursuit of
Moby Dick and Fate and to resign himself to the common lot of
mankind in an imperfect world. The attractions of brotherhood
and peace momentarily conquer his insane desire to storm heaven.
But his good resolves disappear, and he determines to press on in
the chase. Unable to resist the urge to strike at Fate and, by
striking, to probe the universal mystery, he dooms himself.

Ahab as captain of the *Pequod* acts as moral and intellectual
leader of a crew representing every aspect of human life. Among the
strangely assorted collection of characters are primitive savages like
Daggoo and Queequeg, sailors from all the countries of Europe,
young innocents like Pip and Ishmael, wise old seafarers, men of
different religious faiths, good men and bad men. Some, like
Stubb, laugh at life; others, like Starbuck, prize devotion to duty.
The ship meets in the course of its voyage a great many other
whaling ships bound on their own courses and intent on their own
concerns. The meetings at sea provide interesting interludes in the
story, sometimes humorous and sometimes tragic, but they also
serve to shed the light of numerous and varying points of view on
Ahab's quest. One such meeting demonstrates Ahab's loss of
humanity. When the *Rachel* asks for aid in the search for a lost

whaleboat which contains the captain's only son, Ahab, now close on the trail of Moby Dick, unfeelingly refuses.

One of the minor characteristics of the book that modern readers may regard as a defect is the use of melodramatic devices to inspire fear or wonder. Although Melville's literary principles in 1850 were edging more and more toward scientific realism, he introduced into the story, either through habit or in a bid for popularity, such relics of eighteenth-century taste as the Parsee Fedallah and his mysterious companions. These odd creatures, having for no apparent reason stolen aboard the ship secretly and in the darkness, remain hidden for months below decks and are not seen until called out as the special crew of the captain's whaleboat after the White Whale has been sighted. While the reason for Fedallah's presence in the book may lie, as Thorp suggests, in the fact that he symbolizes the evil which Ahab has created for himself[19]—an evil spawned by single-minded hatred—yet as an actor in the drama he is nearly unbelievable. He must be considered a throwback to the phantom figures that haunt the shadowy stairways of gothic horror tales, or the grim underlings of Milton's fallen Satan. Fedallah predicts, accurately though in ambiguous terms, the death of Ahab; and he apparently relishes the wrong interpretation that the mad captain places on his words. Everything turns out as he has foretold, but not exactly as Ahab has been led to believe. On the ultimate day of the chase Fedallah is gruesomely beheld by his captain, lashed lifeless by twined harpoon ropes to the revolving body of Moby Dick. Ahab himself, whom—as predicted—only hemp can kill, is dragged into the sea to his death by a coil of rope accidentally looped around his neck just after he has cast his harpoon vengefully into the whale.

When the frantic struggle to finish *Moby-Dick* and see it through the press was finally ended, Melville confessed to his friend Hawthorne: ''I have written a wicked book and feel spotless as the lamb.''[20] While readers today might not consider the work ''wicked,'' nineteenth-century Christianity would clearly regard it so because the chief character openly questions the goodness of God. In his moments of despair Ahab even doubts the existence of a just Creator. Like Satan, he refuses to accept the fact of his inferiority and weakness and generally sees the universe as having been ''formed in fright.'' Melville, in spite of having created such a character and expressed through him some of his own religious and philosophical doubts, could feel personally ''spotless'' and innocent because as author he could hold himself aloof from the madness of Ahab and because he had shown the defiance of heaven to be ultimately self destructive.

In summation, one may say that the several different levels of meaning on which Melville speaks in *Moby-Dick,* baffling as they were to many readers of the nineteenth century, have today been fairly well defined. On one level Melville presents an exciting narrative of adventure at sea; on another, a remarkably accurate account of the American whale fisheries and the whaleman's life. On a deeper level he explores human psychology—still deeper, man's moral nature and his relationship to his universe. To the last-named problem he offers no clear-cut solution but only a powerful *No* to ready-made philosophies and creeds. From the supposition that Ahab in some degree depicts the spiritual autobiography of his creator (though young Ishmael and not Ahab is the actual narrator of the story and thus more closely relates to Melville), one may infer Melville's arrival in 1850 at the "Everlasting No" in the development of a personal philosophy. *Moby-Dick* declares allegorically (as its author did more directly in his letters to Hawthorne) total independence of subservience to any established religious or philosophical explanation of man's role in the universal order. It stands, however dangerously, as a declaration of man's freedom to control his own spiritual destiny. The risks are understood and accepted: "Make it an utter wreck, if wreck I must!" Melville's admiration for Hawthorne as a "Nay-sayer" indicates his own leanings in this direction:

He says No! in thunder; but the Devil himself cannot make him say *yes.* For all men who say *yes,* lie; and all men who say *no,*—why, they are in the happy condition of judicious, unincumbered travellers in Europe; they cross the frontiers into Eternity with nothing but a carpet-bag—that is to say, the Ego. Whereas those *yes*-gentry, they travel with heaps of baggage, and damn them! they will never get through the Custom House.[21]

To his deep disquiet, however, as the perspicacious Hawthorne was to observe later, Melville never could be comfortable in his unbelief.[22] To describe the state of his mind revealed in *Moby-Dick,* one may use the words he applied in his famous review of *Mosses from an Old Manse* to the author of that collection of thoughtful tales and call him "a seeker, not a finder yet."

IV   *Narrative and Myth*

Once we begin to recognize in *Moby-Dick* the supreme statement of Melville's "Everlasting No," the story takes on a fascination it could never have as a straightforward narrative of adventure at sea, however heroic in proportions, or as a partly fictional account of whaling and cetology. Its philosophical undercurrent as well as its frequently noticed resemblance to the great myths of western culture and folklore help to explain the difficulties often encountered in a first reading of the story and, on the other hand, its appeal to the whole complex of biological memories and social urges that form an element in every man's racial inheritance. For the reader who does not insist upon classifying *Moby-Dick* strictly in one literary category or another, its rereading can be endlessly fresh and revealing. How the various ingredients of this masterpiece are mixed and how they balance and support each other to produce a single but multifaceted effect can be seen in part from an examination of the way in which the plot of this unusual narrative unfolds.

The story begins on a winter's day in the city of New York, where a young American—he calls himself Ishmael, after the half-Egyptian son of Abraham and Hagar who was driven from his home and wandered in barren lands—low in funds and low in spirit, in desperation decides to seek his fortune aboard one of the whaling ships he knows to be signing crews for voyages to the Pacific Ocean. The name Ishmael sems appropriate for him not only because he feels alone and foresaken but also because it fits the whaling crews of the nineteenth century, which were composed largely of the dregs and scum of maritime life—true outcasts from society. Traveling to New Bedford, Massachusetts, the chief whaling port of the United States, Ishmael stops for two nights at the Spouter Inn, where he makes his initial acquaintance with men who earn their living by killing whales. They prove a strange lot. Strangest of all to Ishmael is the cannibal Queequeg, a savage harpooner from the South Seas with whom he unwillingly finds himself sharing a bed. The savage, however, turns out to be harmless and even amiable; after some humorously depicted moments of terror, Ishmael accepts him as a bosom companion. They agree to go job-hunting together and to sign aboard the same ship.

On a Sunday, following the ancient custom of seamen preparing to start on a dangerous voyage, Ishmael and Queequeg attend church at the Whaleman's Chapel, where they hear Father Mapple, a noted preacher, deliver a sermon on Jonah. The first of two remarkable sermons in *Moby-Dick,* this one in a sense proclaims the real theme of the book. Looming high above his motley congregation in a pulpit shaped like the prow of a whaling ship, Father Mapple employs the language of seafaring men as he explains the message of the Old Testament fable.

"Shipmates," he declares, "this book, containing only four chapters—four yarns—is one of the smallest strands in the mighty cable of the Scriptures. Yet what depths of the soul does Jonah's deep sealine sound! What a pregnant lesson to us is this prophet! What a noble thing is that canticle in the fish's belly!" He proceeds to tell the story, to discuss Jonah's perverse disobedience of God, and to relate the ensuing misadventures during the storm and in the stomach of a large fish. He brings out what he considers to be the main lesson of the tale in these words:

> But *what* is this lesson that the book of Jonah teaches? Shipmates, it is a two-stranded lesson; a lesson to us all as sinful men, and a lesson to me as a pilot of the living God. As sinful men, it is a lesson to us all, because it is a story of the sin, hard-heartedness, suddenly awakened fears, the swift punishment, repentance, prayers, and finally the deliverance and joy of Jonah. As with all sinners among men, the sin of this son of Amittai was in his wilful disobedience of the command of God—never mind what that command was, or how conveyed—which he found a hard command. But all the things that God would have us do are hard for us to do—remember that—and hence, he oftener commands us than endeavors to persuade. And if we obey God, we must disobey ourselves; and it is in this disobeying ourselves, wherein the hardness of obeying God consists.

The sermon admirably foreshadows Ahab—who, like Jonah, stubbornly disobeys the will of God; though, unlike Jonah, he does not seek refuge in a hiding place but openly defies God—and points a warning of the consequences of disobedience.

On Monday, Ishmael and Queequeg sail on a little packet schooner to Nantucket, the island far-famed as the birthplace of modern whaling, where, after a night at the Try Pots (that serves fish at all meals), they sign for a long voyage aboard the *Pequod,* a doughty old whaling ship headed for the South Pacific. They are enrolled as members of the crew by two parsimonious elderly Quakers, Captain Peleg and Captain Bildad; but they are unable to meet the ship's commander, Captain Ahab. When they inquire about their future captain, Peleg describes him as a renowned whalehunter whose leg recently has been bitten off by a large bull whale. He explains further:

I know Captain Ahab well; I've sailed with him as mate years ago; I know what he is—a good man—something like me—only there's a good deal more of him. Aye, aye, I know that he was never very jolly; and I know that on the passage home, he was a little out of his mind for a spell; but it was the sharp shooting pains in his bleeding stump that brought that about, as any one might see. I know, too, that ever since he lost his leg last voyage by that accursed whale, he's been a kind of moody—desperate moody, and savage sometimes; but that will all pass off. And once for all, let me tell thee and assure thee, young man, it's better to sail with a moody good captain than a laughing bad one. So good-bye to thee—and wrong not Captain Ahab, because he happens to have a wicked name. Besides, my boy, he has a wife—not three voyages wedded—a sweet, resigned girl. Think of that; by that sweet girl that old man has a child: hold ye then there can be any utter, hopeless harm in Ahab? No, no, my lad; stricken, blasted, if he be, Ahab has his humanities!

This rather unexpected and impassioned plea for Ahab may be more disturbing than reassuring, but Ishmael and Queequeg take it as a matter of course and are soon busy with preparations for the sailing scheduled for a few days hence.

During this interim period, a ragged stranger stops them on the wharf one morning and in mysterious words and gestures tries to warn them against sailing aboard the *Pequod*. He tells them his name is Elijah. This incident arouses apprehensions, but they brush off the warning as a sailor's prank. In the murky dawn on the day of sailing they catch a momentary glimpse of several shadowy figures going on board the ship, and Elijah mysteriously materializes again to hint that these figures will be nowhere in sight when the two shipmates enter the *Pequod*—a prediction that oddly proves correct. Despite these ominous portents, Ishmael and his cannibal companion join the rest of the crew for duty. With Captain Ahab still not in evidence, the *Pequod* weighs anchor on Christmas Day and sets out upon her fateful voyage.

V   *Men and Whales*

The story gives us now, after a brief transitional chapter (23) on the desire of the human soul for independence of thought (symbolized by Melville in life on the wild sea), an interesting description of the whaling industry in general and its importance in world history, after which follows an introduction to the officers and crew of the *Pequod.* Chief among the dramatis personae gathered on this floating world-in-microcosm are the courageous and sensible Starbuck, first mate; the easy-going Stubb, second mate; Flask, pugnacious and jolly, the third mate; and the harpooners—Queequeg, Tashtego (a Gay Head Indian), and the Negro savage, Daggoo.

Only after the ship has been at sea for several days does Captain Ahab at last appear on the quarter-deck—a tall, broad, powerful man of late maturity who seems "made of solid bronze." Though healthy and vigorous, he displays two terrible deformities: a whale-ivory leg to replace that slashed off by the whale and a livid scar extending from his hairline down his cheek and neck and apparently streaking the entire length of his body. On his face and in his whole aspect he shows the signs of an inner anguish. There is, Ishmael observes, "a crucifixion in his face," and he looks "like a man cut away from the stake." Though inwardly tortured, Ahab rules the ship with an iron hand, and he leaves no doubt regarding his feeling of innate superiority over his men. When Stubb approaches him to complain that the noise of the ivory leg pacing across the quarter-deck at night keeps the sailors below decks awake, Ahab spurns him with a contemptuous insult: "Down, dog, and kennel!" Ahab's bitter mental discomfort and his burning dedication to the real purpose of the voyage (unannounced as yet) are shown, however, when he deliberately throws overboard his beloved pipe, the solacing companion of happier days. Both acts of rejection (first of Stubb, then of the pipe) seem to symbolize Ahab's determination to shut himself off during his quest from brotherhood with humanity and from all material comfort.

The story is interrupted (chapter 32), as it is frequently throughout the book, by scientific information about whales and whaling. Drawing freely upon Scoresby and Beale,[23] among others, for cetological details, the section treats of whales in lighthearted fashion, humorously classifying them on the basis of size; but the data given are surprisingly accurate. Fortunately, Melville's facts come from reliable scientific sources and not from hearsay or the personal observations of an untrained sailor lad. Chapter 35 may indeed be drawn from personal experience; for it reveals in moving terms the thoughts and emotions of a man at the masthead.

The highly reflective and quiet chapter precedes one of the most exciting, dramatic scenes in the book. Assembling his entire crew before him on deck, Ahab reveals to them the secret mission of this voyage. Rather than attempting to capture as many whales as possible until the hold is loaded with oil, they are to search for and help to kill a particular whale—the albino bull Moby Dick whose jaws destroyed the captain's leg. By skillful psychological appeal, including the offer of a reward for the first sighting of Moby Dick, the ritualistic blessing of the harpoons, and the drinking of toasts in rum to the whale's eternal destruction, Ahab easily wins over the crew to his plan for vengeance. Only Starbuck remains unenthusiastic about the wisdom of such a revenge and about the feasibility of pursuing a particular whale across an immense ocean.

To Starbuck, the only person aboard whom he holds in much esteem, Ahab explains that the search has another meaning. It entails more than blind vengeance on a brute of the sea; it is a deliberate protest against the sharkish nature of the world and against man's weak subjugation to fate. Believing himself to be held unfairly in a spiritual prison by the powers of nature or the Creator, Ahab rashly proposes to "strike through the wall" of his prison symbolically by murdering the White Whale, who is in Ahab's eyes the evil agent that caused his dismemberment. Horrified at such blasphemy, Starbuck opposes but cannot halt his captain's mad quest. He begins to realize that Ahab is at least partially insane. Meanwhile, enlivened by the rum, the crew dance upon the deck at midnight, while Starbuck laments the purpose of the voyage and Ahab gloats over the successful broaching of his wild plot.

Ishmael, now committed by his own choice to a part in Captain Ahab's revenge, comments upon Moby Dick and the many legends told about him, devoting a chapter (42) to whiteness as a symbol of terror and evil. After more discussion of the cruising habits and physical strength of the whale and some intricate philosophical musings regarding fate, Ishmael describes excitedly what happens when the first whale of the cruise is sighted.

VI *Whale Hunt*

"There she blows! there! there! she blows! she blows!" Tastego shouts from the masthead, and instantly the whole ship is galvanized into action. In the midst of preparations for lowering the whaleboats, from which the harpooning is done, a dusky group of Parsees appear as if miraculously upon deck. Their presence in the ship has been vaguely suspected but never actually acknowledged until now. They are the shadowy phantoms glimpsed by Ishmael and Queequeg in the misty dawn of the sailing day. Until now they have remained hidden to act as the special crew of the captain's whaleboat. As four boats are lowered and sailors leap into them, the dangerous and strenuous game of hunting down the whale and of harpooning and lancing him begins. The thrilling events leading up to a "Nantucket sleigh ride" are graphically described in ringing terms. In this case the whale, which turns out not to be Moby Dick in spite of Ahab's hopeful anticipation, manages to escape.

The *Pequod* now cruises for several weeks in the Atlantic, moving southward among the whaling grounds toward the Cape of Good Hope, where its course will turn eastward. When another ship is met, the first question from the *Pequod* is always, "Have ye seen the White Whale?" Although the passing *Albatross* provides no news, a gam among the officers and crews of the *Pequod* and the *Town-Ho* offers information about Moby Dick and an interesting sailors' tale. The story, supposedly true, tells how a treacherous man is killed by the white whale in a manner that strongly suggests the hand of God punishing him for his crimes.[24] The gam offers a welcome respite from the labors and boredoms of sailing, but mention of Mody Dick makes Ahab eager to be on his way. After Ishmael's description of the gam, his narrative is broken off, and there follows a discussion of whale pictures and of the whale's eating habits, with a short chapter (60) on the rope used in capturing whales.

In the Indian Ocean several weeks later, on a warm, calm, and sleepy day, Ishmael and his fellow watchers at the masts with startling suddenness catch sight of a gigantic sperm whale and erupt the tidings in unison. Immediately the boats are lowered, and after some fine heroics, the whale is killed and brought alongside the ship. The following day the back-breaking work of stripping off its blubber, trying-out the oil, and storing the product in oaken casks below decks occurs. During the night, high-living Stubb, whose boat crew claims credit for the actual capture of the whale, orders Daggoo to cut a steak from the floating carcass and has the Negro cook prepare a midnight supper. Stubb eats the steak, done rare, with much gusto, though pretending to be annoyed by the noisy sharks that feed all night upon the dead whale's body.

Losing patience at last, Stubb in an ironic jest commands the cook to preach a sermon to the sharks. This abbreviated sermon—the second in *Moby-Dick*—is to persuade the splashing sharks to a more Christian conduct. Philosophically, the sermon casts important light on the deeper layers of Melville's meaning in the book. Further, it shows that the Darwinian concept of nature had already replaced romantic notions of nature's friendliness in Melville's mind.

The Negro, forced against his will to entertain the mate in a manner calculated cynically to shock his own religious inclination and thus embarrass him, to Stubb's amusement, applies to the sharks the very terms of censure that he would like to direct at Stubb and the human race in general. After a peroration, the main body of the sermon is delivered as follows:

> Your woraciousness, fellow-critters, I dont blame ye so much for; dat is natur, and can't be helped; but to gobern dat wicked natur, dat is de pint. You is sharks, sartin; but if you gobern de shark in you, why den you be angel; for all angel is not'ing more dan de shark well goberned. Now, look here, bred'ren, just try wonst to be cibil, a helping yourselbs from dat whale. Don't be tearin' de blubber out your neighbor's mout, I say. Is not one shark dood right as toder to dat whale? And, by Gor, none on you has de right to dat whale; dat whale belong to someone else. I know some o' you has berry brig mout, brigger dan oders; but den de brig mouts sometimes has de small bellies; so dat de brigness ob de mout is not to swaller wid, but to bite off de blubber for de small fry ob sharks, dat can't get into de scrouge to help demselves.

"Well done, old Fleece!" encourages the highly amused mate—and adds ironically, "That's Christianity."

Fleece decides to break off the sermon, complaining of the feeding sharks, "'Dey don't hear one word; no use a-preachin' to such dam g'uttons as you call 'em, till dare bellies is full, and dare bellies is bottomless." At Stubb's final urging, he bestows the benediction: "Cussed fellow-critters! Kick up de damndest row as ever you can; fill your dam' bellies 'till dey bust—and den die."

The relationship of the second sermon to the first, Father Mapple's charming discourse on Jonah, is clear. In each of the sermons the members of the congregation are cautioned by the preacher to resist their own impulses and control their selfish desires. The earlier sermon specifically advises obedience to the will of God. The second shows rather more awareness of the man-of-warrishness of nature, the tendency of all creatures to prey upon one another. This awareness of the cruel struggle for existence in the natural world, so different from the unrealistic views of the romanticists, is further emphasized in what Ishmael-Melville calls the whale's "funeral." He depicts the "sea-vulture" sharks feasting upon the corpse "all in pious mourning," the "air-shark" vultures overhead "all punctiliously in black or speckled." Both regard the funeral as a gratuitous banquet, and the narrator comments: "Oh, horrible vulturism of earth! from which not the mightiest whale is free."

The *Pequod,* having loaded its oil and allowed the skeleton of its victim to sink below the waves, continues its voyage with fresh vigor, occasionally meeting other ships and securing various reports of Moby Dick. Here and there in the book, additional chapters are inserted that supply detailed materials on the subjects of cetology and the customs of whaling. As one whaling ship after another is encountered, the reports indicate that slowly but steadily the *Pequod* is closing in on Moby Dick. The nine different ships that the *Pequod* consults or gams with during the voyage mark the rising tension of the chase while adding fearful evidence of the ferocity and cunning of the great maverick whale. The symbolism used by Melville in identifying these nine ships also has a definite bearing upon the development of the outward and inward narratives of the book.[25]

The first ship, the *Albatross,* named for the sailors' favorite bird of good omen, passes by (as mentioned above) without pausing and in doing so somehow gives the impression of impending evil instead of good fortune. When the crew of the *Town-Ho* gams with men from the *Pequod,* the story told by the former carries the broad hint that Moby Dick may be considered an agent for the justice of heaven. Radney's death in the story, asserts Ishmael-Melville, strikes the simpleminded sailors as "a certain wondrous, inverted visitation of one of those so-called judgments of God which at times are said to overtake some men." The gam with the *Jeroboam* provides a second brief tale which may be interpreted as a foreshadowing of Ahab's doom. On board the *Jeroboam* is a violent Shaker fanatic who believes himself to be the archangel Gabriel and who has warned his captain against attacking Moby Dick. The whale, he says, is God incarnate; thus hunting him is blasphemy. A mate of the vessel, having disregarded Gabriel's dire warnings, has been killed in an odd manner by the White Whale while attempting to harpoon him. Gabriel confidently foretells a like fate for anyone daring to challenge the whale's divinity—as Ahab, of course, intends to do.

When the *Pequod* meets the *Jungfrau,* the latter's German captain proves to be ignorant of Moby Dick and also somewhat ignorant of whaling skills in general. His innocence and ineptness permit the *Pequod's* more experienced crew to defeat him in a contest over the capture of a large bull whale; and his virgin ship is last seen, to the vast merriment of his Yankee rivals, lowering her boats to pursue a swift and uncapturable finback. The *Rose-Bud,* or *Bouton de Rose,* is a French whaling ship that has captured a sick and odoriferous whale. Realizing that the bloated whale contains prized ambergris, the wily Stubb succeeds in cheating the unwary French captain of the carcass by offering to tow it away. In the *Samuel Enderby,* a British vessel, Ahab chats with a captain who has lost an arm to a sperm whale; but, eschewing any thought of revenge, the Englishman refuses to regard the accident as anything more than a normal risk of his trade. He sees no point in encouraging Ahab's purpose by giving him anything more than the barest information about his last sighting of Moby Dick. The reasonableness of the British captain contrasts markedly with Ahab's monomania.

The *Bachelor* is a happy ship that has had excellent luck in the whaling grounds and now, with hatches filled, looks forward contentedly to the homeward journey. Ahab finds the captain and crew of this vessel "too damned jolly" for his own mood and rapidly parts company. "Call me," he says, in a tone of contempt for the gay and heavily loaded *Bachelor,* "an empty ship, and outward bound." The *Rachel* approaches the *Pequod* looking for help in trying to locate a lost whaleboat containing, among the boat crew, the captain's only son. Here is an opportunity for Ahab to show his humanitarian spirit and to put aside his personal quest in order to do a good action. The *Rachel,* however, discloses that it has had sight of Moby Dick within the preceding twenty-four hours. As soon as Ahab hears how close he is to the object of his long search, he can think of nothing else. Firmly, albeit with a rueful and apologetic air, he refuses the plea for aid and pushes forward in the relentless pursuit of his nemesis. The *Delight,* the last ship encountered by the *Pequod,* is (like some of the others) ironically misnamed. There is nothing happy about her; for she has recently sighted and attacked Moby Dick and bears on her deck the shattered hulk of one of her whaleboats to prove it. The boat crew has presumably perished. Her "hollow-cheeked" captain dolefully affirms as his earnest belief the opinion that "the harpoon is not yet forged" that is capable of destroying the White Whale. In spite of this clear and terrible warning, Ahab rushes on.

VII *End of the Chase*

Shortly after the *Pequod's* gam with the *Samuel Enderby* (chapter 100), during the course of which Ahab has learned the direction in which his quarry was last seen heading, events in the story have begun to move with increasing speed, though temporarily interrupted by some discussions regarding the vast size of the largest whales. Departing abruptly from the British vessel, Ahab has accidentally splintered his ivory leg and therefore finds it necessary to have a substitute constructed by the ship's carpenter. In an impressive soliloquy he remarks upon the irony of his indebtedness to the simple but efficient craftsman—whom he calls "man-maker"—for a limb to stand on. The carpenter, largely unimpressed by these philosophical ramblings, concerns himself only with producing a good piece of work. Later, the same capable worker in wood builds a coffin at the request of Queequeg, who is stricken with a fever and certain that his end has arrived. Queequeg eventually recovers, but his coffin remains on deck to serve after the sinking of the *Pequod* as a lifesaving buoy for Ishmael.

In a tense dramatic scene (chapter 113), Ahab consecrates to his insane vengeance the special harpoon, forged by the ship's blacksmith from the steel of razor blades, intended solely for the capture of Moby Dick. This harpoon is tempered in blood from the veins of the three savage harpooners on the *Pequod* and blasphemously blessed by Ahab in the name of the Devil in words that some critics regard as the real motto of *Moby-Dick*: "*Ego non baptizo te in nomine patris, sed in nomine diaboli!*" The act boldly symbolizes the mad whaleman's defiance of God.

Ahab further sunders himself apart from the world when he grows unreasonably angry over the limitations of the mechanical quadrant by which he has been navigating. "Foolish toy!" he cries, "babies' plaything of haughty Admirals, and Commodores, and Captains; the world brags of thee, of thy cunning and might; but what after all canst thou do, but tell the poor, pitiful point, where thou thyself happenest to be on this wide planet, and the hand that holds thee: no! not one jot more!'' This function, for Ahab, is far from enough. Determining to navigate by dead reckoning only, he throws down the quadrant and angrily tramples it. In this rejection Ahab symbolically rejects the wisdom of science and condemns it as insufficient for solving man's great spiritual problems. Ahab's general scientific knowledge, of course, is considerable; and he makes use of this knowledge to his advantage when flaming corpusants form in the rigging of the ship during a storm and when the compass needle goes awry. In a manner awesome and mysterious to his crew, he grounds the static electricity of the corpusants and magnetizes a bit of steel for a compass needle.

Now, as the ship approaches nearer and nearer to that spot in the Pacific Ocean where the White Whale is cruising alone, the signs of impending tragedy begin to accumulate. The tone of the narrative turns more ominous. With his personal crisis imminent, Ahab rather unexpectedly befriends little Pip, the Negro boy who has been driven into insanity by fright. Pip has been destroyed by the hardheartedness of the world. Having had the misfortune to tumble out of a whaleboat in the heat of the chase, he has discovered in utter bewilderment that his fellowmen are more willing to abandon him to his death on the ocean than to give up their chance to capture a financially promising whale. Ahab senses a kind of kinship in madness between himself and Pip. His own form of madness drives him to defy and attack the nature of the universe; Pip's response to the cruelty of his fate is to accept it passively and without complaint or gesture of retaliation. The welling of his unavoidable sympathy for Pip, so helpless in the hands of the gods, arouses a protective instinct in Ahab.

This feeling and the consequent emergence of a sense of brotherhood nearly cure Ahab of his monomania. He watches over the boy and comforts him, and in so doing is drawn closer to the recognition of his own humanity and of the need of all creatures for understanding and love. As he begins to identify himself once again with the rest of humankind, to be no longer solitary and aloof, his interest in his single-minded quest gradually subsides. He actually permits himself, under the urging of the sensible Starbuck, to think of home and family and nearly to acquiesce in ordering an about-ship (chapter 132). He almost agrees to relinquish his passion for vengeance on Moby Dick. At this point in the story Ahab reaches to the very edge of the pit into which he has fallen and is ready to pull himself up to salvation, but long habit (or fate) prevents it. On the following day the distinctive odor of whale, wafted across the waves to his quick nostrils, finally overpowers all his favorable resolutions. His wild hatred revives; forgetting all else, he commands full sail in the direction of the White Whale.

The chapters which bring *Moby-Dick* to its close are among the most vividly written in all the world's literature. Though not likely to be fully appreciated without the background of the preceding scenes in the book, they are frequently excerpted and printed as a unit in literary collections. They describe with steadily mounting excitement the long-awaited sighting of Moby Dick and the vigorous but fruitless attempts to capture and kill him over a period of three stirring days. On the first of these three days the White Whale escapes by seizing Ahab's whaleboat between his jaws and snapping it into splinters. Ahab is very nearly killed in the skirmish but is rescued in the nick of time when the *Pequod* sails directly upon Moby Dick to drive him off. In the darkness of that night the track of the whale is temporarily lost; the next morning, after some frantic searching, his characteristic spout is again discovered. On the second day the whale tangles the harpoon lines together and overturns the boats, dashing their crews into the sea among the sharks. Ahab's whalebone leg is broken off, and his evil genius, Fedallah, disappears. On the final day of the chase Fedallah's body reappears, fastened by twisted lines to the body of the whale. This discovery serves as a tragic omen for Ahab; Fedallah has previously foretold that Ahab's death will follow his own. He has also assured his captain, however, that the latter will never be killed except by a hempen rope. This part of the prediction, which has given Ahab a false feeling of confidence, comes true on the third day when, after Ahab's harpoon has been cast with every ounce of strength and hate into the whale, the singing rope loops itself around the great whale hunter's neck, dragging him in a flash out of his boat into the churning wake of Moby Dick, to inevitable destruction.

His death follows the most thrilling and horrifying incident in the book. Enraged by the persistence of his enemies, with several barbed harpoons painfully imbedded in his huge body, the White Whale savagely turns upon the *Pequod* itself, ramming it at full speed with his tremendous head and sinking it with all its crew. The lone survivor of the sudden catastrophe is Ishmael, who finds himself solitarily floating upon the barren waters, buoyed up ironically by Queequeg's coffin. In an epilogue the narrator tells of his rescue two days later from the sea and the strangely indifferent sharks by the whaleship *Rachel,* still cruising the area in a vain hunt for its lost whaleboat. The strayed boat and its crew are never located; instead, says Ishmael, the ship, "in her retracing search after her missing children, only found another orphan."

Thus the most famous voyage in American literature ends in overwhelming tragedy—the "total wreck" that Ahab consciously preferred over submission to human fate.

VIII   *A Rural Bowl of Milk*

Pierre, like *Moby-Dick,* displays numerous traces of Melville's fondness for Shakespeare. A balcony scene opens the story; and, as in *Moby-Dick,* there are dialogues and soliloquies in dramatic form. If *Moby-Dick* may be called Melville's *Lear* or *Macbeth, Pierre* is his *Romeo and Juliet* or *Hamlet*—even to the point of ending with its chief characters lying dead in a tragic heap. *Pierre,* however, differs in so many respects from either *Mardi* or *Moby-Dick* that one might hesitate at first glance to include it in the trilogy. A second glance quickly reveals its direct connection with Melville's philosophical quest. At the risk of oversimplification, one might say of *Mardi* that it poses the question, "What is Truth?"; of *Moby-Dick* that it attacks the same question from another side by asking, "What is Fate?"; of *Pierre* that it deals with still another aspect of the problem by its concern with a third question, "What is Virtue?"

Pierre is alone among Melville's novels in having no maritime setting. All the action takes place in the delightful countryside of wealthy estates near Saddle Meadows (presumably the Berkshire Hills of Massachusetts) and in the city of New York. Pierre Glendinning, only son of an affluent and haughty widow, is just emerging from his teens as the story begins. His prospects appear ideal; for, besides being of excellent family, he is talented, handsome, financially secure, and beloved by the beautiful and virtuous Lucy Tartan, to whom he has recently become engaged.

In the midst of this Eden, Pierre suddenly finds himself vis-à-vis a dreadful dilemma by making the acquaintance of an attractive young woman in a neighboring village who claims relationship as his half-sister. According to her story, she is the illegitimate offspring of his father and a French mistress. Pierre, upon hearing her claims, is thunderstruck. How is it possible for him to believe that his revered father, whose memory Mrs. Glendinning cherishes as well-nigh sacred and whom Pierre has been taught since boyhood to regard as morally perfect, was guilty not only of adultery but also of the more heartless crime of abandoning his own daughter to poverty and obscurity? Doubt and suspicion shake Pierre to his foundations. He recalls various ambiguous remarks of his father's intimates—and especially a certain portrait of his father—that suggest the existence of a hidden chapter in his father's life. Gradually Pierre lets himself be convinced of the validity of Isabel's claims, and he decides to accept her as his older sister.

Now the main problem of the story presents itself: How can Pierre, as a virtuous and honest person, protect Isabel without causing injury to others? What course of action can he adopt which will be just and fair to all concerned? If he acknowledges Isabel openly, he will tarnish his dead father's reputation and probably break his doting mother's heart. If he rejects Isabel, he will be withholding from her dishonestly her place in society and the protection of money and family that rightfully belong as much to her as to him. The only method he can hit upon to solve the problem is to sacrifice his own happiness to hers. He determines to give up Lucy, whom he loves dearly, and to pretend that he has married Isabel. By this maneuver he can provide assistance and recognition to his half-sister without blemishing his father's memory.

When Pierre announces his pretended marriage, his mother promptly disowns him. He flees with Isabel to the city, where he seeks help and comfort from his cousin Glen Stanly, a close boyhood friend with whom he has exchanged promises of eternal loyalty. But Glen, who has now fallen heir to the Glendinning fortune and is leading a gay life in high society, insolently disavows him. Spoiled by his rearing in luxurious, comfortable security, Pierre hereupon faces the cold necessity of earning a living for himself and Isabel. Having previously won praise for his talents as a writer, he undertakes to write a novel—an experience totally different, when he is doing it under financial pressures, from the pleasant, leisure-time occupation it has been in the past.

As the weeks go by, Pierre begins unexpectedly to realize that his true feeling for his half-sister (and hers for him) is not one of mere brotherly affection but of sexual attraction. Were his motives in protecting her as pure, then, as he had originally believed? Pierre at first evades the question, horrified at the thought of incest; but he gives way grudgingly to his passion. Later, when evidence appears

that throws a serious doubt upon the supposed guilt of his father
and thus upon the basic reasons for Pierre's actions, he has to ask
himself whether what he has done is really justified by the facts.
But a deeper question occurs to him. Has he acted from truly virtuous motives or because of his secret, unconscious physical desire
for Isabel?

Lucy, meanwhile, forgiving Pierre for his treatment of her and
sensing his reasons, moves to the city against the wishes of her
family and joins the household of the runaways. Her brother and
Glen Stanly publicly denounce Pierre as a traducer, and almost
simultaneously the publisher for whom Pierre has been writing his
book accuses him of swindle and refuses to publish it. Instead of
being a popular novel, as promised, the publisher complains, it is
nothing but a "blasphemous rhapsody." (This recalls to mind Melville's experience with *Mardi*.) All his hopes blasted, Pierre goes
berserk, murders his cousin, and is thrown into prison. Upon learning of Isabel's real (or pretended) identity, Lucy falls dead at his
feet; in desperation, Pierre and Isabel take poison together.

IX   *Problems of Composition*

Though in its later stages one of the most violent and bloody of
Melville's works, *Pierre* may well have been intended as a tale of
domestic passion imitating some of the bestsellers then current.
Melville was probably quite in earnest when he described it in his
letter to Sophia Hawthorne, soon after the book was begun, as a
"rural bowl of milk." In 1852 Melville's principal aim was to win
both a steady income and literary fame; and, recognizing that his
works must be entertaining if they were to be widely read, he had
already shown his willingness to suppress his tendency toward
philosophical discussion and to woo readers by certain literary
compromises. Following the warning he had received in the public's rejection of *Mardi,* he had chosen the path of expedience by
writing straightforward stories of adventure in *Redburn* and in
White-Jacket. In *Moby-Dick,* encouraged by a kind of literary
trickery learned from Carlyle, he had edged perilously close to the
allegorical style which the public detested; but the composition of
his masterpiece had been accomplished only after a prolonged and
wearing struggle. His letters to Hawthorne about *Moby-Dick* not
only hint strongly of his great apprehension regarding its reception
by readers but show that he had exerted considerable effort to keep
it from being another *Mardi.*

There is good reason, therefore, to believe that, at the time he launched into the writing of *Pierre,* Melville did not clearly see where his favorite habits of thought were going to lead him. The once widely held theory that Melville wrote *Pierre* deliberately to agitate the critics who had attacked his *Moby-Dick* neither has any firm evidence to support it nor makes the least kind of sense. In fact, the first half of the book plainly imitates the popular fiction of the nineteenth century. Since both its mood and style seem entirely foreign to Melville's nature as well as to the theme developed later in the book, much of the earlier portion appears contrived and ineffective.

Melville may actually have used as a model such a work as *The Foresters,* by John Wilson (the famed "Christopher North" of *Blackwood's Magazine)*—a book enthusiastically admired by British and American readers between 1825 and 1850 and reprinted numerous times. A copy of the 1846 edition was in the personal library of Melville's close literary acquaintance, James T. Fields.[26] *The Foresters,* according to its author, was written to demonstrate "the superior excellence and happiness of virtue" over wealth, social position, and self-seeking. The scene is rural Scotland, and the chief characters are Lucy Forester, her parents and friends, her Aunt Isabel, and her two sweethearts. There is also a Cousin Martha who, like Isabel in *Pierre,* spends her childhood in an orphanage and is forced to work as a servant girl because of a crime committed by her father before her birth. The plot consists of a harrowing series of misfortunes borne with Christian fortitude and resignation by members of the Forester family, but all ends happily.

The second half of *Pierre* sounds almost like a deliberate protest against the kind of sentimental nonsense presented in *The Foresters.* Pierre's adherence to virtuous principles leads him only to misfortune. Did Melville, then, write his book entirely as a satire on the romantic novel, or did he begin by attempting to imitate it, only to change his mind in midstream? The answer is not easy to determine, but the second alternative appears the more likely. Until the point at which Pierre scans the ambiguous Plinlimmon pamphlet and begins to write his novel, the story could easily be another version of *The Foresters.*

From this point on, however, it changes markedly. Instead of taking the easy and certainly more popular course of pursuing Pierre's misadventures to a final happy conclusion, Melville apparently could not resist his inclination to probe the moral problem of Pierre to its depths. With nearly visible pain, he starts Pierre off on a search for truth. He shows his hero beginning the quest with optimism and good cheer, only to find his picture of truth and virtue becoming progressively darker and more blurred; in the end his quest casts him into despair and bitterness. The nadir is reached when Pierre sees himself in his dreams as the giant Enceladus imprisoned on the Mount of Titans, throwing his armless body as a battering ram against the cliffs in a futile assault upon impregnable heaven. Like Ahab, Enceladus-Pierre feels that his human weakness weighs him down and prevents his attainment of the universal center of truth. All his decisions, therefore, must be made in the darkness of human ignorance, knowledge itself proving for man frighteningly masked and ambiguous. The metaphysical character of the second half of *Pierre* is further indicated by the novel's unusual subtitle, "The Ambiguities."

The modern reader can understand *Pierre* best if he divides the plot into three phases. In the first phase, Pierre's ideas about virtue are definite and noble; he is absolutely clear in his mind as to the path he must follow. This phase ends when he is disowned by his mother and leaves with Isabel (accompanied by Delly Ulver, a disgraced girl whom he rescues from shame) for the city. The second phase opens when Pierre accidentally finds and reads the dilapidated Plotinus Plinlimmon pamphlet, "Chronometricals and Horologicals," in which pure virtue is declared inappropriate for human society and a practical compromise, or "virtuous expediency," is recommended.[27] By studying the pamphlet and by applying its principles to his own case, Pierre is led slowly to question the moral standards by which he has acted. The third phase occurs near the end of the book when Pierre belatedly sees that passion instead of high-principled virtue has unconsciously motivated his interest in Isabel. During this final phase he examines an ambiguous portrait, reminding him of his father's, in which the subject's character may be read in totally different ways. Pierre now understands that he may have been wrong in accepting too readily the uncertain evidence of his father's guilt. If his father was guiltless and if Isabel is not really Pierre's half-sister, the virtuous young man has caused himself and others a vast amount of suffering in vain. The true answer to his question, *What is Virtue?* remains horribly in doubt.

While Melville's presumed change of plan in the composition of *Pierre* killed any chance the book had of becoming popular, it resulted in what may reasonably be called the first native novel of psychological realism. Besides raising grave misgivings about one of the favorite romantic notions of the nineteenth century—that virtuous conduct always leads to final good—the book also delves into the basic motives of human behavior. A noble and well-intentioned man, it implies, can act upon motives of a mysterious origin whose operation upon him he does not even recognize until too late. How, then, can anyone do right or achieve justice? Is man bound by internal forces beyond his ken?

Melville had previously produced in *Typee* the first novel of South Seas romance and in doing so had started a whole new vogue in romantic fiction.[28] The vogue has flourished charmingly ever since. In *Pierre* he introduced another important literary trend—that of psychological analysis. He may thus be credited with having begun two distinct new movements in the development of the American novel. To readers of his own day, of course, only the first of these innovations appeared commendable. Perhaps because it struck too close to home, they were made uncomfortable by an exploration of the unconscious. They preferred in their fiction to see virtue and evil as clearly defined opposites; and they regarded any close attention to the secret motivations of conduct—especially that of sex—as indecent if not heretical.

X   A Note of Hope

Viewed separately, *Mardi, Moby-Dick,* and *Pierre* constitute three successive statements of Melville's "Everlasting No" to the creeds and philosophies of his time. Viewed as a trilogy, they reveal a remarkably full picture of Melville's metaphysical thinking at the most productive period of his life. They probe and analyze the nature of truth, fate, and virtue without arriving at any affirmative answers to the questions asked. *Mardi* allegorically teaches a negative doctrine when its hero fails after an exhaustive search to attain his goal of absolute knowledge, but it also asserts the independence of the human soul in Taji's refusal to capitulate by abandoning his quest. *Moby-Dick* skillfully submerges the allegory but retains enough explicit symbolism to express Melville's *No!* in a voice of thunder. *Pierre,* after what may be regarded as a nonphilosophical digression in an attempted reproduction of the popular sentimental novel, gets back on the metaphysical track as its hero begins to examine the realities of his beliefs in order to solve a practical moral problem. In *Pierre,* as in the two earlier novels, the honest quest for truth brings bitter frustration and a savage protest from the hero-victim.

Not one of the three novels ends, however, without a strong note of hope. Taji, having searched the world of Mardi in vain, enters the afterworld with a gesture of exultation. In *Moby-Dick* a part of heaven is carried symbolically into the maelstrom of the sinking ship when Tashtego inadvertently fastens the living eagle to the *Pequod's* mast as a plume of indomitability. In *Pierre,* man's unconquerable spirit of inquiry is beautifully symbolized in the flowers that cover his frustration: "[E]ven so, to grim Enceladus, the world the gods had chained for a ball to drag at his o'erfreighted feet;—even so that globe put forth a thousand flowers, whose fragile smiles disguised his ponderous load."

CHAPTER 7

Long Decline

I The End of Fame

AFTER THE FAILURE of *Pierre*—one possibly more surprising to him than the failure of *Mardi*—Melville's ambition to capture fame as an author noticeably began to subside. Furthermore, it seems very likely that he had nearly exhausted the stock of ideas and experiences upon which he had been drawing for the narrative skeletons of his books. Had the American public responded with any show of enthusiasm to the satirical allegory in *Mardi* or to the psychological realism in *Pierre*, Melville might have been flattered into relying more fully upon his powerful imagination. Since readers preferred either maudlin sentiment or exotic adventure and seemed appalled by any violation of literary convention, he instead acquired a sense of disgust with public taste and a feeling that the adulation of the masses might not be worth trying to win. "To go down to posterity is bad enough, any way," he had confided in a letter to his friend Hawthorne only a year earlier, "but to go down as a 'man who lived among the cannibals'!"[1]

Nevertheless, he did not entirely give up the game. He needed money; and, besides, writing had become for him a personally rewarding if intellectually painful occupation. But not surprisingly, many of Melville's prose works after 1852 reflect a consciousness of man's ingratitude to man, of the tragic inconsistencies and hypocrisies in human conduct, and of the total emptiness of worldly fame. Such a reflection is seen in the story of *Israel Potter* (subtitled "His Fifty Years of Exile"), which was taken almost bodily from Henry Trumbull's pedestrian little book about a soldier in the American Revolution who suffered a long captivity abroad. The plot clearly had struck an echoing chord in Melville's heart shortly after the publication of *Mardi,* and five years later he rewrote the brief tale competently and effectively, making such alterations as

113

pleased him in the interest of sharper dramatic appeal.[2] The portraits of such famous American heroes as Benjamin Franklin, Ethan Allen, and John Paul Jones are exhibited in what Melville doubtlessly conceived to be a more honestly realistic manner than is common among historical romances. Despite its inadequacy as history and some carelessness of composition, *Israel Potter* shows generally good workmanship and, while never as greatly admired as Melville's major works, has had its own special circle of avid readers. The fact that a Philadelphia publisher was willing to go to the trouble of pirating it may in itself be a compliment of sorts.

Besides his main source for the story, Melville gained verisimilitude by consulting various biographies of John Paul Jones, Ethan Allen's *Narrative* of captivity, Nathaniel Fanning's *Narrative of the Adventures of an American Naval Officer,* and a history of Berkshire County. Ostensibly a story (one of the last of its type) catering to the spirit of intense nationalism rampant in America during the decades following the Revolutionary War, the book also contains many aspects of the tradition of comic folklore which was gradually becoming a part of respectable American literature and which reached its acme in the brilliant writing of Mark Twain.

Carefully avoiding open criticism of nineteenth-century society and all weightily philosophical comments, Melville took for his principal theme the popular saying of Poor Richard, stated at least three times in the book: "God helps them that help themselves." Israel, the hero, is a typically self-reliant Yankee—stubborn enough to persevere in the face of suffering and danger; cunning, honest, sometimes brave; and never wholly defeated. A farm boy and woodsman who has taken to the sea, he leads in youth a life of high adventure that is changed by fate into one of unhappy drudgery in a foreign land. He returns in old age to die forgotten among the hills that gave him birth.

Some of the most interesting chapters are those describing Israel's meetings with the shrewd and worldly-wise Franklin; the wolflike and unprincipled Jones; and the bluff and brawny Westerner, Allen. Of the smooth-mannered Franklin, Israel comments: "Every time he comes in he robs me, with an air all the time, too, as if he were making me presents." To the innocent but perceptive young Yankee, Franklin is revealed as a suave but sharp-dealing man of business who puts his own welfare above most other considerations. Equally ambitious and self-centered, but without Franklin's gentlemanly air, is the reckless Jones—courageous, but a savage at heart. Only Allen, among these famous men, wins Israel's (and Melville's) approbation as a representative of the great heart of America. Convivial, frank, hearty in manner, but able to dissemble by assuming a barbaric exterior when exhibited as a captive to British curiosity seekers, he embodies the indomitable spirit of the frontier.

As usual, Melville seems at his best in those portions of the novel dealing with life at sea. The two chapters describing the battle between the *Bon Homme Richard* and the *Serapis,* with Israel at one point hurling grenades from the yardarm into the hatchway of the enemy vessel, are perhaps the most exciting and vivid in the book. Preferring truth and realism to patriotic fervor, however, Melville gives an account of the battle (as he does of the other historical incidents and personages) that is more balanced and objective than many of those current in the nineteenth century.

II   *Tales and Sketches*

Before publishing *Israel Potter,* the first installment of which came out as a Fourth of July story in *Putnam's* during the summer of 1854, Melville had been kept fairly busy producing several shorter pieces for magazines. Those appearing in *Putnam's* prior to January, 1856, he subsequently collected in a single volume which he entitled *The Piazza Tales.* (Richard Fogle has provided a very useful introduction to these and Melville's other tales and sketches.)[3] The *Piazza Tales* includes "The Piazza," an essay written especially for the collection; "Bartleby," "Benito Cereno," "The Lightning-Rod Man," "The Encantadas," and "The Bell-Tower." Of this group at least three — "Bartleby," "Benito Cereno," and "The Encantadas" — can be called major examples of their genre.

"Bartleby" has always enjoyed a certain amount of popular approbation and within recent years has been successfully dramatized and broadcast over television. The strangely moving tale of the scrivener who stubbornly asserts his individual freedom of choice by refusing to conform to society's rules but whose defiance is quiet and passive rather than vigorously active has long tickled the fancy of readers who probably had no idea why they were so pleased by it. To most readers, Bartleby possesses the attractiveness of a highly unusual character; despite his unsociable attitude and his irritating stubbornness, he inspires a feeling of pity rather than disgust. By defying the world unobtrusively he manages to accomplish—his method closely resembling Thoreau's "passive resistance"—what many others would like to do if they dared. Passive self-assertion ultimately requires as much courage as an opposition to the world's ways openly announced; though, as Melville suggests, people are likely to mistake passive heroes for nonentities.

To Bartleby's employer, narrator of the tale, he serves as a source of bewilderment and concern because of his utter lack of the customary human ambitions and vices. The employer is a goodhearted, "safe" man in the world's eyes and by accepted moral standards. Thus to him anyone who makes no move to seek personal advantage and who expresses disapproval of this man-of-war universe by simply withdrawing from it and preferring to take no part in its activities appears nothing less than a freak. He tries every appeal he can think of to break down Bartleby's reserve, but without avail; and at length, not for the reasons he rationalizes but because Bartleby's mere presence pricks his conscience, he discharges the scrivener from his employ. Bartleby, in his mild way, frustrates this attempt at getting rid of him by merely staying on. Finally, in desperation, the employer moves his offices. Yet Bartleby's plight continues to prey on his mind; in the hope of respite, the narrator takes a trip out of town.

On his return, he finds the scrivener in prison, where he sits quietly looking at the walls. Making no complaint but impervious to any arguments for self-preservation, Bartleby stops eating and very shortly dies. His death is an unobtrusive one, wholly without the crashing wreckage and violence of Ahab's; yet each has asserted himself as a sovereign individual — the one by active and the other by passive defiance of his fate. The narrator, judging Bartleby by his own code of morals, recognizes that the scrivener is not evil and is puzzled and made uneasy at heart by passive resistance, the cause of which he only dimly discerns. In the end he can do no more than feel sorry and vaguely crushed by his memory of the man who, given freedom of choice within the limits of human action, preferred simply to choose nothing.

"Benito Cereno" also presents the case of a "passive resister"—though in this tale *helpless* might be a better word—who is so appalled by the blackness of the world that he withdraws from it in fear. This is not to assert that "Benito Cereno," in spite of certain similarities, follows the same theme as "Bartleby." "Benito Cereno" is a story in which a perfectly normal, active man, Captain Delano of the *Bachelor's Delight* (strikingly like the employer-narrator in "Bartleby"), meets and observes but is entirely unable to understand the strange behavior of Don Benito Cereno, who has been utterly cowed by the horror of a tragic experience in a life hitherto pleasant, carefree, and well-ordered.

The tale is constructed much in the same dichotomous pattern as that employed by Poe for "The Gold Bug." There are two distinct parts to the story, each important, each giving a separate view of the same events, or one part presenting a mystery and the other the solution. Melville's tale, however, is not one of ratiocination but of psychological probing into man's nature. The plot opens in the harbor of an uninhabited island off the coast of Chile, where an American sealer is anchored in 1799. A Spanish merchantman, the *San Dominick,* appears on the scene sailing erratically and obviously in some sort of trouble. Delano decides that the stranger needs help and generously goes on board, only to discover an amazing situation. The *San Dominick* is carrying a cargo of Negro slaves, but she has had so rough a voyage that by gales, fever, and scurvy she has lost most of her officers and crew. Cereno, captain of the vessel, is an elegant young man grown haggard from the misfortunes of the voyage. He maintains little discipline and even allows the blacks (excepting a chained giant, Atufal) to run freely about the decks. His chief assistant appears to be his complaisant Negro body-servant Babo, who remains with him every moment, like a faithful dog.

But Captain Delano cannot shake off the feeling that something is terribly amiss aboard the slaver. Benito Cereno alternates in his manner between an ingratiating but unintelligible friendliness and a cold, almost insulting aloofness. The white sailors are few and are constantly surrounded by bevies of blacks. The ominous Atufal, though in chains, makes his appearance mysteriously in various parts of the ship. While strongly affected by the sense of mystery and incipient nightmare, the good-natured American captain finally decides that his fears and suspicions are groundless and starts back to his own vessel. With alarming abruptness, Benito Cereno suddenly leaps overboard from the *San Dominick* into Captain Delano's boat; Babo, with a dagger in his hand, leaps after him. Baffled at first and believing that Babo is trying to save his master, Delano at last sees the truth: Babo's real intention is to murder Cereno. This realization explains everything; for it means the slaves have revolted and captured the ship, killing most of the whites.

After saving the Spanish captain, the Americans recapture the *San Dominick* and sail with her to Lima, where the case is laid before the viceregal courts. In the second half of the story, which now follows, Benito Cereno listlessly—and in a sense unwillingly—gives an official deposition of the facts. He tells the brutal story of the revolt, and he reveals the primitive cruelty of the blacks, led by Babo. In their hatred of their former captors, the slaves have hung at the bow of the ship, as a figurehead, the skeleton of their owner, Don Alexandro Aranda, the close friend of Benito Cereno; and under it they have written, as a warning to all whites: "Follow your leader."[4] After the trial Benito Cereno retires to a monastery and soon dies. The head of Babo, placed on a stake in the public square of Lima, continues to look threateningly in the monastery's direction. The symbolism here is plain: Cereno cannot escape the memory of earth's evil nor the recognition of nature's vulturism. It becomes even more plain in the parting words between Cereno and Captain Delano, who tries to cheer him up. "You are saved," says Delano encouragingly. "What has cast such a shadow upon you?" "The Negro," replies Benito Cereno, and this is all that he will say.

Although some critics have denied the greatness of "Benito Cereno" as literature, perhaps proving that preconceived social theories can blind even a brilliant person to artistic excellence,[5] no reader can begin the story without at once recognizing its power. Rosalie Feltenstein has conveniently summarized the general critical opinion by praising "the architectural skill with which the story is constructed" and by asserting that "there is not one careless, useless, weak, or redundant touch in the whole tale."[6] That Melville borrowed his plot from Amasa Delano's *Voyages* is, of course, well known.[7]

"The Encantadas" consists of ten haunting sketches of the Galapagos Islands that may have been written originally as part of the book on tortoises which Melville planned for Harper and Brothers. While each of the sketches comprises an independent unit, together they contribute effectively to a single, overall impression. *In toto,* they paint the gray picture of a world cursed and made barren by its own vulturism, a world rendered bearable only by patience and courage. Ostensibly the sketches describe the islands—their appearance, geography, history, flora and fauna, and legends. Through symbolism the reader also sees aspects of the universe in microcosm and the consequences of evil. (Melville hints in his journals and poetry at the surprising and suggestive resemblance between these dead islands and Palestine, home of three great religions.) The islands are first regarded (sketches 1 and 2) as a group, next (sketches 3 and 4) in perspective, as viewed individually in their watery setting from the Rock Redondo and close at hand from the harbor entrance near Narborough to Albemarle, the largest island, the other twenty-three smaller islands fading off into the distance. The narrow escape of the United States frigate *Essex* from wrecking on Redondo is described (sketch 5), and the use of Barrington Isle by buccaneers is discussed (sketch 6) in lighter vein. Then follow three sketches telling stories of outcasts on the various islands, with a final sketch commenting on these and quoting at the end the epitaph on the grave of a castaway. Most interesting and moving of the sketches is the pathetic story of Hunilla, a Chola woman, who suffers hopeless isolation and brutal rape after the accidental drowning of her husband and brother but endures her martyrdom with a noble dignity like that of Agatha in the Nantucket incident which Melville outlined for Hawthorne. Strange to say, Melville manages to invest the barren Galapagos Islands—those "five-and-twenty heaps of cinders"—with a lurid fascination almost impossible to resist.

III   *Satirical Voyage*

In *The Confidence-Man* Melville again strikes the borders of allegory. American readers of his day did not like the book; indeed, he barely succeeded in getting it published. The work as a whole seems to have been concocted by putting together a loosely bound series of ironic sketches (perhaps originally planned for serialization in *Putnam's*) which deal with man's gullible yet suspicious nature and with "the mystery of human subjectivity." The passengers on a Mississippi River steamboat begin on April Fool's Day (significantly) a voyage which turns into a variegated masquerade of human foibles; for the steamer *Fidèle* is the stage on which the individual acts are played. One can hardly avoid the impression in reading the book that Melville set himself to write a playful farce and that only inadvertently did the bitter undertone of his plot assume the ascendancy. Instead of smiling indulgently at the follies he depicted, Melville betrayed by a grimace his horror at the hypocrisy that engenders them. His mood being bitter, his wit became acrid and stinging. Instead of poking satirical fun at the inconsistency between man's professed beliefs and his actual conduct, as the first chapters appear to promise, *The Confidence-Man* hammers at human weakness with a savage but anguished satire. In essence the book amounts to a psychological analysis of human character, the allegorical spotlight centering on its moral ambiguities.

Early in the river voyage a crippled Negro dressed in white lamb's wool (the crucified Lamb?) emerges among the passengers urging them to display charity toward one another. As the voyage proceeds, he returns in other guises but invariably proves to be a cunning confidence man who succeeds in winning people's trust in order to cheat them. Nearly every incident or discussion that ensues is really a separate essay on the theme of charity and brotherhood. Neither the swindlers nor the swindled are granted much sympathy on the part of the author, who indirectly argues that an attitude of suspicion offers no better protection against the chicanery of life than an attitude of trust. Besides the main action, several shorter tales are inserted here and there; they take up such matters as the tragedy of an honest, good-hearted merchant forced by his wife's termagant nature into beggary; the sufferings of a witness in a trial who is held in jail while the murderer goes free; the exploits and self-justification of a notorious Indian hater; the unsuspected heroism of a bankrupt who adopts the shield of pretended misanthropy until he has regained his fortunes and can reappear among his friends as a social equal; and the sad experience of a young candlemaker who unwillingly accepts a loan from a generous friend, only to be ruined when the friend's true character asserts itself.

People in *The Confidence-Man* generally prove to be different from what they seem. A congenial fellow who praises wine is revealed as distrustful and a teetotaler. An Emersonian transcendentalist preaches love and spiritual friendship while exhibiting cold aloofness toward his fellow passengers; and his young disciple shows by practical reasoning how it is possible to keep "one eye on the invisible" and "the other on the main chance." A cynical barber with a "No Trust" sign is easily hoodwinked and cheated. An old man who earnestly insists that he relies entirely on the protection of God buys a special set of locks, probably worthless, as a necessary protection against thieves.

The book as a whole provides a rather bitter commentary on human gullibility and self-deception. It presents life as an ambiguous confidence game in which humanity professes one set of principles and lives by another. It may also be read as a faintly humorous commentary on talkative, attractive swindlers and their willing dupes during the enthusiastic period of American westward expansion—a subject not uncommon in mid-nineteenth-century magazines (witness Poe's "The Diddlers" and others). Artemus Ward, the famous humorist who was a contemporary of Melville, frequently made confidence men the object of scorn. "The real enemy of mankind, as [Artemus Ward] saw it," remarks a recent critic, "was plain old humbug, usually preceded by 'Thus saith the Lord' or 'Thus saith the expert' or thus saith something other than one's own God-given common sense."⁸ Melville adopted the literary convention already familiar to readers of his time but failed in making the treatment humorous.

The setting of *The Confidence-Man,* like that of other works by Melville, represents the human race in microcosm aboard a ship—this time a river vessel. The voyage allegorizes the journey of life itself. Mark Twain employed a similar device and a similar theme with somewhat greater skill in *The Adventures of Huckleberry Finn.* The incorrigible Huck serves as the unifying character for a series of picaresque experiences along the river. Melville's confidence man, while ostensibly one character appearing at various times in various guises (some critics believe him to symbolize either God or the Devil), seems hardly a single individual but several and thus lacks the cohesive power to give the novel effective unity.

IV   Theories of the Novel

Three chapters in *The Confidence-Man* (chapters 14, 33, and 44) take up Melville's theories regarding the writing of novels. They show his growing preference for scientific realism as against imaginative romanticism. He finds absurd the attitude of some readers who presumably read novels to escape the dullness of their lives but who insist upon a literal, factual description of events. Purely reportorial writing, says Melville, cannot reveal the real

truth about life; and fiction should present "more reality than real
life itself can show." The novelist must not be false to nature, but
he must work in a fictional world "unfettered, exhilarated, in effect transformed."

Equally absurb to Melville is the notion that a character in a
novel, unlike persons in real life, must be completely consistent.
"That fiction," he warns, "where every character can, by reason
of its consistency, be comprehended at a glance, either exhibits but
sections of character, making them appear for wholes, or else is
very untrue to reality." Scientists of the mind (psychologists) condemn as mere "sallies of ingenuity" attempts to "represent human
nature not in obscurity, but transparency." He has little use for
those novelists who cleverly spin "the tangled web of some character, and then raise admiration . . . at their satisfactory unravelling
of it." The true-to-life character is neither consistent nor
transparent, and the deeper mysteries of his being may never be
fathomed.

Melville remarks further upon the common misunderstanding of
what makes a character in literature truly original. It is not, he
avers, the traits that stamp a character as either eccentric or
unusual. Certain personal attributes may be startling or even
unique, but they affect only the particular character himself;
whereas the true "original" in literature must affect by his
attributes all his associated characters and the environment in
which he acts. He must be a great individual, a person who matters
to others and himself. ("No great and enduring volume," he says
jokingly in *Moby-Dick,* "can be written on the flea, though many
there be who have tried it.") The essentially original character "is
like a revolving Drummond light, raying away from itself all round
it—everything is lit by it, everything starts from it (mark how it is
with Hamlet), so that, in certain minds, there follows upon the
adequate conception of such a character, an effect, in its way, akin
to that which in Genesis attends upon the beginning of things."

V   *The Poetry*

Melville became a poet, as Thomas Hardy did, late in his literary
career. Never a great poet, he wrote some verse which displays
a thoroughly respectable fluency and structural competence.
Reversing the common and admittedly preferable custom of
serving an apprenticeship in poetry before turning to prose, he
found the labor of shaping his complex and frequently ambivalent
thoughts to forthright lyrical form vastly difficult when he had

once lost the confident glibness of youth. It is not easy to escape the conclusion, when reading his verse, that lack of adolescent practice in poetical composition accounts for a certain stiffness and a seeming absence of spontaneity. Much of the material is labored, with scars of the workmanship still showing.

While indications exist that Melville experienced in his teens the customary and natural interest in sentimental versifying, there is no evidence pointing to a serious concern with poetical creation before 1859. Even the occasional rimes appearing in *Mardi* (1849), which were the earliest of his poems to be published, function in the novel almost entirely as ornaments for humorous relief. Though they may suggest that young Melville possessed a musical ear, such doggerel as

> We fish, we fish, we merrily swim,
> We care not for friend nor for foe:
> Our fins are stout,
> Our tails are out,
> As through the seas we go. . . .

can hardly be dignified with recognition as true poetry; nor was it so intended. Somewhat resembling the songs in the comedies of Shakespeare, these poetic interpolations introduce largely meaningless but entertaining music, less for the sake of the plot than for variety and noise. A few of them sound like parodies of their Shakespearean prototypes. Witness the song beginning

> Oh! royal is the rose
> But barbed with many a dart;
> Beware, beware the rose,
> 'Tis cankered at the heart. . . .

and the smoking song,

> Care is all stuff:
> Puff! Puff!
> To puff is enough:—
> Puff! Puff!
> More musky than snuff,
> And warm is a puff:—
> Puff! Puff!
> Here we sit mid our puffs,
> Like old lords in their ruffs,
> Snug as bears in their muffs:—
> Puff! Puff!
> Then puff, puff, puff

For care is all stuff,
Puffed off in a puff.—
Puff! Puff!

Such happy effusions of lyrical nonsense attract by their youthful gaiety and facility of expression. They are songs to be sung and then forgotten, uncomplicated by deep or somber thought; they celebrate the superficial moment of innocent exuberance, adventurous excitement, or bibulousness.

Far different are the poems of Melville's maturity. Nearly every stanza of his later work betrays the signs of intense artistic struggle—of struggle, moreover, in which the artist was not always victorious over his materials. Some traces of the earlier poetic style with its reckless humor, giddy rhythm, and fondness for the mouthing of words do indeed appear in the poems written by Melville during his more settled years. In such a poem as "The Maldive Shark" (published in *John Marr and Other Sailors),* for example, there can be detected a surface current of bubbling humor; but the mood now suggests rather the amusing smile than the frank laughter of "We Fish, We Fish." "The Maldive Shark" is intertwined with frightening realism:

About the Shark, phlegmatical one,
Pale sot of the Maldive sea,
The sleek little pilot-fish, azure and slim,
How alert in attendance be.
From his saw-pit of mouth, from his charnel of maw
They have nothing of harm to dread,
But liquidly glide on his ghostly flank
Or before his Gorgonian head;
Or lurk in the port of serrated teeth
In white triple tiers of glittering gates,
And there find a haven when peril's abroad,
An asylum in jaws of the Fates!
They are friends; and friendly they guide him to prey,
Yet never partake of the treat—
Eyes and brains to the dotard lethargic and dull,
Pale ravener of horrible meat.

If the poems in *Battle-Pieces* and *John Marr* are compared as a group with the ornamental verses in *Mardi,* it becomes apparent at once that two significant changes occurred in Melville's view of poetry during the decade or so just preceding the Civil War. The first of these entails the transformation of his view from one in which poetry is regarded as a device to delight the senses—as almost exclusively entertainment in the form of beautiful description, musical sound, and humor—to one in which it serves as the vehicle for serious philosophical contemplation and the author's profoundest strictures upon life. The song in *Mardi* that begins "We drop our dead in the sea, The bottomless, bottomless sea . . ." presents a charming picture of ocean burial with hardly a trace of any consciousness of death or emotional responsiveness. It simply has no depth. On the other hand, "Shiloh: A Requiem," composed in commemoration of the bloody battle fought in April, 1862, combines beauty of image and phrase with profound thought and feeling; it obviously was written for a purpose other than pure entertainment.

> Skimming lightly, wheeling still,
>   The swallows fly low
> Over the field in clouded days,
>   The forest-field of Shiloh—
> Over the field where April rain
> Solaced the parched ones stretched in pain
> Through the pause of night
> That followed the Sunday fight
>   Around the church of Shiloh—
> The church so lone, the log-built one,
> That echoed to many a parting groan
>   And natural prayer
> Of dying foemen mingled there—
> Foemen at morn, but friends at eve—
>   Fame or country least their care:
> (What like a bullet can undeceive!)
>   But now they lie low,
> While over them the swallows skim,
>   And all is hushed at Shiloh.

Such a poem, whatever its technical defects (the riming, for instance, of "fly low" and "lie low" with "Shiloh"), clearly means to convey philosophical ideas and emotional undercurrents and not solely the flights of poetical fancy. As with his prose, Melville seems with his verse to have started by trying to entertain and to have ended by striving to teach.

The second change in Melville's view of poetry, closely related to

the first, is from optimistic romanticism to psychological realism.
In form, nearly all his poetry follows the conventional pattern of
the writing popular in his own time. The structure, except for a few
notable experiments, is that of the romantic nature poets and the
Elizabethans; it is admirably suited to the subject matter of
romanticism but poorly designed for the kind of realistic analysis
of human life that Melville and his poetic successors were learning
to make. Perhaps herein lies much of the secret of Melville's general artistic failure in poetry. Whitman, faced by a similar problem,
boldly invented new forms and encompassed his forward-looking
ideas and fresh images of life in patterns unhampered by the traditions of rime and meter. When he wrote in the conventional romantic mode (as in "O Captain, My Captain"), he had almost as much
difficulty as Melville. Had the latter sensed in time what he could
have learned about poetic technique from Whitman, instead of
relying for his patterns upon Shakespeare and the romantic lyricists
of the nineteenth century, he might have become a far better poet.

Robert Penn Warren, arguing that Melville never succeeded in
mastering his craft, calls him "a poet of shreds and patches"[9] and
by this presumably means that Melville's work is uneven, with a
mixture of brilliant and pedestrian lines. He picks fault not so
much with Melville's ideas and images — many of which he finds
impressive — as with his cramped manner of writing. This criticism
appears eminently just and can be supported by numerous examples from the poetry. Yet it must be owned that Melville's best
efforts in verse are well worth reading — if not for what he
achieved, then for what he attempted. A dozen or two of the poems
in quality rank very high indeed, and a collection of these would
make a thorougly readable short book.[10]

During Melville's day his only poems receiving any currency consisted in a handful of the patriotic Civil War pieces — especially
"Sheridan at Cedar Creek," "Chattanooga," "The March to the
Sea," "The Cumberland," and "Gettysburg" — and these retain a
certain degree of popularity today. Not many of his contemporaries
recognized in Melville a "Brady of Civil War verse"[11] or saw that
he had written in *Battle-Pieces* "a short poetic history of the
war."[12] The modern reader, unreceptive to romantic enthusiasm or
sentiment, is more likely to prefer other pieces or to find stimulation in deeper aspects of Melville's poetry: the stubborn probing
into human motives and revelation of human character, the search
for philosophical truth, and the somewhat clumsy experimentation

with form to express the ideas of a new age rapidly turning toward science.

Recent critics who have selected favorite poems from among Melville's works betray a preference for those denoting an attitude of pessimism. This preference may reveal more about the critics' minds than about Melville. True, any thoughtful writing regarding the great and bitter war which formed the subject of Melville's first book of poetry must necessarily be permeated with a tone of sadness. Taken as a group, however, the poems in *Battle-Pieces, John Marr,* and *Timoleon* show less of personal pessimism than they do of humanitarian sympathy for suffering and of hope for a better world. Such a poem as "Misgivings, 1860," which declares that

> Nature's dark side is heeded now —
> (Ah! optimist-cheer disheartened flown) —
> A child may read the moody brow
> Of yon black mountain lone. . . .

presents only one facet of Melville's mood. Other pieces, including the supplement in prose at the end of *Battle-Pieces,* express not only the horror of man's behavior to man but — more positively — a definite advocacy of "Progress and Humanity."

Among the poems likely to prove most interesting to modern readers are "Donelson," which describes in highly dramatic and unusual style the reactions of citizens to the war bulletins; "Malvern Hill," which with its elm trees imperviously observing human self-destruction foreshadows Carl Sandburg's "Grass"; "Bridegroom Dick," a lament for old seamen, which constitutes a kind of "Ballade for Dead Ladies" with a mood of quiet resignation; "After the Pleasure Party," a poem on love; and such little vignettes as "The Returned Volunteer to His Rifle":

> Over this hearth — my father's seat —
> Repose, to patriot-memory dear,
> Thou tried companion, whom at last I greet
> By steepy banks of Hudson here.
> How oft I told thee of this scene —
> The Highlands blue — the river's narrowing sheen.
> Little at Gettysburg we thought
> To find such haven; but God kept it green.
> Long rest! with belt, and bayonet, and canteen.

Melville wrote a surprising amount of poetry after his conversion to the poetic mode at the age of forty. Collections that include *Battle-Pieces, John Marr, Timoleon,* and the verses left in manuscript at his death make a substantial volume, and to this quantity *Clarel* adds two additional volumes. While the loss of all his verses would probably detract nothing from the stature of Melville as an American writer, critics and students of literature can be grateful to the poems for what they reveal of a great writer's moods and ideas during a trying period of his life. Mumford suggests, for instance, that Melville's absorption in poetry and the stimulation of events in the war had the effect of drawing him out of the introverted and morally skeptical mood which had produced *The Confidence-Man.*[13] The war gave him a sense of personal involvement, so that his writings began to reflect a more definite stand on moral issues and a preference for concrete action over abstract contemplation.

VI   *The Pilgrimage*

Clarel, the first carefully edited modern edition of which has only recently been published,[14] is important chiefly for its detailed revelation of Melville's intellectual peregrinations in his continuing search for philosophical certainty and religious faith. Thorp calls this long poem the key to Melville's thought in his later years.[15] Underlying its complicated arguments that present nearly all the accepted points of view respecting religion is a graver issue — the question of whether the Christian-Hebraic tradition can endure in the face of scientific realism. By the latter years of the nineteenth century, the discoveries of science — particularly those of geology and zoology — had pretty well given the lie to any literal interpretation of the story of creation in *Genesis.* Melville was forced like other honest thinkers to make the choice between the opposing claims of science and the church.[16]

More than most other literary men of his day, Melville had prepared himself to reach a decision by reading extensively in the scientific works then beginning to appear in some profusion. As background material for his novels, he had read such widely diverse books — to mention only a few — as William Ellis' *Polynesian Researches,* Good's *Book of Nature,* Carlyle's philosophical essays, Beale's *Natural History of the Sperm Whale,* and probably Chambers' popular *Vestiges of the Natural History of Creation.* From such works he derived a growing respect for science and, whether he willed it or not, the realization of its power to prove most of its claims. He adopted the scientific attitude in practice while deploring the tendency of science to exalt itself as a new religion and, by adulation of the intellect, to atrophize human feeling.

Furthermore, Melville's experience had led him to distrust the romantic optimism preached by the nineteenth-century writers and religionists who assumed the inherent beneficence of God and nature. Melville had observed the base brutality of men and of nature in its uncultivated state. He had been forced into an awareness of the savage tooth and bloody claw that lurk beneath nature's pleasant and smiling surface ("The shark / Glides white through the phosphorus sea"). He had seen also the obvious disparity between Christian principles and the unprincipled conduct of even the most ardent professing Christians. Disillusionment at the bitter and stubborn defense of apparent falsehoods by the organized churches of his time against overwhelming scientific evidence had its effect in impelling him to shout an "Everlasting No" at all established creeds during young manhood. But philosophical speculation, when pursued entirely apart from religious dogma, only brought his thinking up against a blank wall — "and perhaps there's naught beyond." Melville, in his flight from religious faith, went as far as a tentative agnosticism. In the long run, of course, agnosticism has never been a comfortable resting place for the inquiring mind; and for Melville it proved a bed in which he could not rest at all. His journey to the Holy Land in 1857 marked a significant step in his persistent search for a satisfying faith. *Clarel* is essentially the record of this part of his quest.

In this extraordinarily long poem of travel and philosophical argument, young Clarel,[17] an American theological student visiting Palestine, falls in love with the lovely converted Jewess, Ruth. Because, after her father's death, Clarel is forbidden by religious custom to visit her for a time, he sets off on a pilgrimage to the shrines of the Holy Land. Falling in with a group of other pilgrims (all presumably seeking for evidences of religious truth), he travels from scene to scene observing, discussing, debating. The pilgrims embody various creeds and attitudes — Derwent, Church of England liberalism; Ungar, Roman Catholicism of the American South; Margoth, science; Nehemiah, blind faith; Vine, uncommitted and reserved individualism; Mortmain, misanthropy; Rolfe, a kind of naturalistic skepticism; and so on. Most of the discussions and arguments revolve around such topics as paganism versus

Christianity, Roman Catholicism versus Protestantism and modernism, science versus religion, and the like. At the end of his journey, Clarel returns to find that Ruth is dead. Readers of the poem by this time, as Mumford points out, have pretty well forgotten her and thus cannot muster appropriate regret at the news of her demise.[18]

Although most of the conversations in the poem simply present alternative arguments and favor no particular conclusions, there is a very clear impression at the close of *Clarel* that Melville has not been attacking Christianity but subtly defending it. The poem does attack, however, the zealots and self-deluded hypocrites of eighteen centuries who interpreted and twisted the plain-spoken teachings of Christ for their own personal glory or gratification, even to the extent of committing outrageous crimes in the name of religion. Melville's concept of Christ as expressed in *Clarel* seems to be this: He was a being who brought mankind the gift of an ideal and of hope that the ideal might be achieved. He blessed mankind with the dream of eventual perfection. While the dream has not yet become realizable, the possibility of somehow attaining it in the future buoys up men's courage, though simultaneously torturing them. Christ as the Ultimate Ideal torments thinking men because they recognize human frailty; that is, man's natural weakness for the present prevents him from reaching the standards of behavior and understanding set by Christ as his goal. Yet the goal remains worth striving for. As Melville counsels his hero in the final stanzas of *Clarel,* each pilgrim should seek to move toward the ideal in the best way he can, even when all direct and convenient approaches may at the moment appear closed.

VII   *The Feeble Yea*

Clarel is both too long and altogether too unpoetic in style ever to attain wide popularity. A narrative poem, it contains more contemplation than action. While anything but careless in composition (in spite of the complaint of at least one early critic to this effect),[19] it clearly contains the kind of literary material which most readers would consider more appropriate for prose than for verse — unless, to be sure, the poet were Milton.

Melville, unfortunately, was no Milton. He was a poet with modern ideas who had not learned modern methods of poetic expression. He wrote in the well-worn romantic idiom of his day, the idiom of Wordsworth, Byron, and Shelley. His efforts to present realistic ideas in hackneyed romantic phrases resulted in much incongruity. Melville's general effect in *Clarel,* then, since he lacked the technical originality of Whitman and the skill of Arnold and Clough, is for his reader a disappointing one. In those portions where matter and form are both romantic in mood, the poem can be briefly charming, but vast sections of it admittedly jar the aesthetic sensibilities. As we have noted, the same failure of technique marred his otherwise commendable poetry on the Civil War. The *Battle-Pieces,* at least, were marked with considerable vigor of expression. *Clarel* somehow gives the impression of a dreary and nearly consistent lassitude of spirit.

The poem opens in a tenor of disillusioned sadness that is maintained through almost the whole work. The first few lines not only establish this mood but offer a fair example of the words and phrasing employed throughout:

> In chamber low and scored by time,
> Masonry old, late washed with lime —
> Much like a tomb new-cut in stone;
> Elbow on knee, and brow sustained
> All motionless on sidelong hand,
> A student sits, and broods alone.
> The small deep casement sheds a ray
> Which tells that in the Holy Town
> It is the passing of the day —
> The Vigil of Epiphany.
> Beside him in the narrow cell
> His luggage lies unpacked; thereon
> The dust lies, and on him as well —
> The dust of travel. But anon
> His face he lifts — in feature fine,
> Yet pale, and all but feminine
> But for the eye and serious brow —
> Then rises, paces to and fro,
> And pauses, saying, ''Other cheer
> Than that anticipated here,
> By me the learner, now I find.
> Theology, art thou so blind?
> What means this naturalistic knell
> In lieu of Siloh's[20] oracle
> Which here should murmur? Snatched from grace,
> And waylaid in the holy place!''

It requires almost a straining of the memory to recall that the meter
used here is the same one dashed off in such a sprightly manner by
Sir Walter Scott in *The Lady of the Lake:*

> The stag at eve had drunk his fill
> Where danced the moon on Monan's rill,
> And deep his midnight lair had made
> In lone Glenartney's hazel shade. . . .

It is an excellent meter for a poem of action but hardly one that
adapts itself readily to the situations and ideas that make up *Clarel.*

The prevailing mood of disillusionment is further strengthened
by the tendency of the main characters to suffer frustration or misfortune. The happy characters are happy in disagreeable or foolish
ways. Margoth delights in destruction; and Nehemiah, probably
the most cheerful and lovable of all the persons in the story, lives in
an unreal world of superstition. Near the end of the poem, in fact,
the poet implies that all creatures appear to be born for suffering:

> In varied forms of fate they wend —
> Or man or animal, 'tis one:
> Cross-bearers all, alike they tend
> And follow, slowly follow on.

The pilgrimage that forms the framework of the story in *Clarel*
is, of course, Melville's favorite narrative device. Nearly all his
novels except *Pierre* describe fateful journeys — usually voyages by
sea. *Mardi,* his earliest novel dealing with a spiritual pilgrimage,
begins in hope and ends in despair; *Clarel* begins in despair and
ends in a vague sort of hope. The reason for Melville's faint and
struggling sense of new hopefulness lies, as William Ellery Sedgwick once perceptively pointed out, in his decision to abandon his
reliance on the intellect as his guide in the quest for heaven.[21] Virgil
could conduct the trembling Dante through hell and purgatory, but
no farther. To ascend the heights required the guidance of Beatrice.
Philosophy having failed him in his attempts to solve the riddle of
the universe, Melville fell back upon faith and love.

He had always asserted that he "stood for the heart"; yet the
fact remains that throughout the late 1840s and 1850s Melville pursued elusive truth chiefly through the agency of mind — with negative results. All the speculative journeys of his previous books had

ended in debacle, so that the limitations of purely intellectual power to solve human problems had become to Melville self-evident. Though the pilgrimage in *Clarel* is directed in substantial degree by Melville's intellect, his growing suspicion of this guide is clearly apparent before the end. Distrust for the head and growing respect for faith mark the bulk of Melville's literary products following the mighty emotional impact upon him of the tragic events and issues of the Civil War.

Led forward exultantly by a keen and robust mind, Melville from about his twenty-fifth year had examined and one by one rejected the standard creeds and philosophies known in his day. Even science, with all its promise, had failed him. He had embraced science with every indication of enthusiasm during the most active period of his life, realizing that it offered a new and realistic approach to the questions that puzzled him, but in many respects it had only deepened his perplexity. In later life he turned against science for what he considered its influence in destroying beauty through cold analysis and ultimately in denying God. In *Clarel,* science is equated with intellect and atheism. Melville's horror is expressed at the thought of

> Man disennobled — brutalized
> By popular science — atheized
> Into a smatterer. . . .

He describes the geologist Margoth (in Derwent's bitter words) in these terms:

> Intelligence veneers his mien
> Though rude: unprofitably keen:
> Sterile, and with sterility
> Self-satisfied.

"Science lights but cannot warm," says Melville, declaring that, while science can add facts to our store of knowledge, it cannot really solve the fundamental mysteries: "Degrees we know, unknown in days before; / The light is greater, hence the shadow more."

To escape despair, Melville was impelled in *Clarel* to turn from science to the faith he found in his own heart. The belief in God in some guise, whether just or unjust, he found necessary to the peace of his soul. He could still ask, with all Nature, "Wherefore ripen us to pain?" Yet, the resigned acceptance of life as it is — the attitude adopted in Serenia — the acquiescence to suffering, and the practice of brotherly love appeared wiser than too much questioning: "Even death may prove unreal at the last, / And stoics be astounded into heaven." When every philosophical system leads to an "Everlasting No," only the heart can answer "Yea."

Clarel, it can be seen, amounts to a definite, though rather tremulous, affirmation in contrast to the powerful negations of Mardi, Moby-Dick, and Pierre. There is no shout of discovery here, but instead a quiet recognition of man's incapacity to live without hope. If the mind's affinity for speculation only succeeds in closing doors, the heart must open them. Despite the horrible vulturism of the natural world and the cruel suffering that every living thing endures, man must retain his aspirations at all costs. No better way has been found, says Melville, than to follow those instincts which raise him above animalism. These are epitomized in "The sign o' the cross — the spirit above the dust!"

Melville's rejection of intellectualism and the emergence of a new point of view, in which the development of trust in the inherent goodness of the human heart and in its potential to overcome evil offers the only hope of reconciliation to suffering, are clearly stated in his parting advice to his student-hero, Clarel:

> Then keep thy heart, though yet but ill-resigned —
> Clarel, thy heart, the issues there but mind;
> That like the crocus budding through the snow —
> That like a swimmer rising from the deep —
> That like a burning secret which doth go
> Even from the bosom that would hoard and keep;
> Emerge thou mayst from the last whelming sea,
> And prove that death but routs life into victory.

CHAPTER 8

Final Flowering

I *Tragedy of Art*

TWO MYTHS regarding Melville's intellectual and literary pilgrimage in the world of ideas remain popular despite a growing accumulation of evidence to disprove them. First, his inner life has been described as utterly tragic. Early Melville scholars deduced from symbolical insinuations in his works and from certain incidents in his life a total mental and spiritual breakdown before the age of forty — caused, presumably, less by overwork than by his insatiable urge to know the unknowable.[1] Secondly, his career as author has been described with uncompromising assurance as a kind of rocket, brilliant but brief in its passage, that hurtled at breakneck speed into the highest reaches of heaven and then, following a spectacular explosion, quietly subsided, burned out and spent, back to earth. According to this view, *Typee* marked the rocket already well off the ground; *Moby-Dick,* the peak of its flight; and *Pierre,* the scattered explosion — the rest being largely silence.

Recent research and rereadings of Melville have shown these judgments to be in the main fallacious. Melville admittedly suffered more than his fair share of hard knocks in life, both as a person and as a writer; and he sank to occasional depths of despair and bitterness just as he rose to heights of overconfident enthusiasm. No consistent pattern of inner tragedy is discernible, however, in his mental and spiritual development. Failure to find his "Yillah" in the quest for absolute philosophical truth did not wreck his mind, nor did it stop him from continuing to write. Long after the alleged "explosion" of his powers in the mighty fiasco of *Pierre* — not a fiasco in every sense, as has been seen — he amply and richly demonstrated his intellectual balance and his abiding faith in his

135

creative artistry by producing such literary triumphs as "Bartleby" and "Benito Cereno."

If any tragedy occurred, it was not one of mind but one of art. The search for truth, with all its inevitable frustrations, may have led him into what seemed a "Solomon's hell"; yet he persisted undaunted and pursued until the end of his days the path he had chosen. On the other hand, lack of understanding and appreciation by his American audience not only daunted but embittered him. While working on *The Confidence-Man,* he must have been painfully aware of his inability to communicate his most cherished ideas to readers in a manner that would win acceptance. In spite of this awareness, he was able to discover no artistically honorable way out of his dilemma. He felt little but shame for such half-hearted compromises with literary and philosophical standards as *Redburn* and *White-Jacket.* The satirical humor that he attempted in *The Confidence-Man* only turned sour and revealed his bitterness. In the last analysis, the one answer he could achieve was the manful suppression of his desire for fame. The effort in time brought a reasonable calm to his flaming spirit; though now and again, as when relatives and friends praised his poetry too extravagantly, the flame burst out anew. A thirst for fame, especially after it has once been fed, is not easy to quench.

That his persistence in the search for elusive truth caused him discomfort may be freely acknowledged; yet the search never entirely discouraged him. Late in life he wrote gently and with a trace of self-disparaging humor about its effect upon him — in a poem he did not publish:

> A Spirit appeared to me, and said
> "Where now would you choose to dwell?
> In the Paradise of the Fool,
> Or in wise Solomon's hell?"
>
> Never he asked me twice:
> "Give me the fool's Paradise."

Despite such a disclaimer, uttered in retrospect, the choice Melville actually made — the choice to which he remained constant throughout his life, even when offered innumerable opportunities to reject it — was not the Paradise of the Fool; and for this we may be grateful. It has been argued rather superciliously that, had Melville attended college, he would have learned there all the standard answers to the standard philosophical questions and thus in his mature years would not have devoted so much of his attention to purely metaphysical problems, however intriguing.[2] If this argument holds, it speaks very ill indeed for a college education, since it implies that the value of institutional study lies in making the mind content. The glory of Melville is his mental *discontent,* which mirrors the attitude of men interested in more than animal materialism and willing to dive deep intellectually. Though largely self-educated, Melville possessed the true philosophical instinct.

He also possessed, however, perhaps to the modern reader's misfortune, an inbred conventionality and a great yearning for social and literary approval. Had he been such a totally defiant individualist as he is frequently painted, he would no doubt have sacrificed home, income, family pride, and reputation in the wild struggle for truth. But this he never did — unless unwittingly. In his books he deliberately compromised with public taste, made strenuous efforts to control and conceal his deeper concerns, and openly imitated the methods of more popularly successful authors — all to no avail. His reading public, having tasted the dessert, had no palate for the main course. Had Melville's audience proved more discriminating and more willing to tolerate his literary experimentation, he might not have been forced into the "personal" writing of his middle years or into seeking what satisfaction he could find within the art itself. A more permissive and open-minded attitude in the United States of his time would have made unnecessary the practically complete submergence of his philosophical and psychological probings to unobtrusive quiescence below the surface of a socially normal, pedestrian, but not unwholesome city-dweller's existence.

There was probably no period at which Melville abandoned writing entirely. Once having taken up the pen, he could never contentedly relinquish it in order to give himself and his thoughts freely to practical matters. No more could he abandon, once he had begun, philosophical and artistic speculation. The rejection of *Mardi* because of its allegorical method (making its readers, after *Typee* and *Omoo,* feel themselves imposed upon) warned him that, if he coveted recognition, he was taking the wrong road. The unfavorable reaction to *Pierre* demonstrated not only that his career as a successful author was dangerously near its close but that he had gone too far down the philosophical road ever to turn back. The new approach (resembling the method of the parable) which he tried in *The Confidence-Man* failed even more inauspiciously, so that he was constrained finally to concede his defeat as a popular author of prose. After *The Confidence-Man* he ceased writing for a general audience and addressed himself to writing for self-release and for the delectation of a small circle of relatives and friends.

The "turning inward" of his literary work was the principal change wrought by lack of public appreciation for his most serious and ambitious works, but another change was effected as well. This consisted of reversion to the romantic mode of expression represented by his turning to lyric poetry. From an artistic as well as a practical point of view, this new tack may have been a mistake; though there is reason to think that Melville felt considerable optimism about his chances for success as a poet. Certainly his courage in attacking a literary field in which he would be judged by different — perhaps even more critical — standards betokens his reluctance to desert the career which had opened for him with so much promise and for which he believed himself best fitted. The resurgence of his literary hopes may have seemed justified when *Battle-Pieces* appeared between covers, but he was nevertheless prepared by his previous failures for the near silence that greeted this event. The book's appearance created no splash but only a few modest ripples.

Clarel he frankly acknowledged in advance as a work "not calculated for popularity." In the latter poem he devised for himself, though not without signs of struggle, an attitude of patience and semiresignation. Content now to forego literary fame, he still persisted in his philosophical quest. While clearly displaying a sense of spiritual uneasiness and lack of certainty, the poem contains a glimmer of hopefulness. Though the attainment of absolute philosophical and religious truth seems no nearer in *Clarel* than in *Mardi,* Melville suggests in it an eventual *rapprochement* between heavenly and worldly truth. Only by clinging firmly to this hope, he persuaded himself, can a thoughtful man bear the terrors of life.

II *The Innocent Sacrifice*

The theme broached in *Clarel* is pursued with firmer certainty and vigor in *Billy Budd,* the last important literary and philosophical statement of Melville's career. This book, fortunately, he wrote under excellent conditions — without the fierce twin pressures of money and fame under which Melville had worked in his youth.

Only the pressure of time remained. Realizing that his nearly un-bounded energies of former days had now "sensibly declined," as he put it, he faced, like Mozart, the prospect of having his time run out before he could complete his task. Yet he seems to have labored with quiet assurance and unhurriedly at his final novel, changing his mind at intervals regarding details of its composition, and obviously concerned almost wholly with pleasing himself. Writing with no public in mind — except, perhaps, that of the future — he could indulge his habit of probing the secret wellsprings of human behavior. He could produce with consummate artistry a parable of human sacrifice gentle in its tone and yet savage in its depiction of spiritual and social wickedness.

Considered as the work of a man in his seventies, *Billy Budd* strikes the reader as amazing; but it would be amazing in any case. Its dignity of manner is equal to that of Milton in *Samson Agonistes*. In certain respects — for example, in its clear mastery of literary technique — it has been ranked by some on a higher level than even *Moby-Dick,* although in bulk it is less impressive and in mood less violent. Instead of the rebellious outcry against Fate's injustice that gives *Moby-Dick* its Promethean character, *Billy Budd* offers only acquiescent submission to necessity; but it points to man rather than Fate as the perpetrator of the tragedy. The story moves its readers in strong though subtle ways and clearly deserves to stand with his other acknowledged masterpieces (*Moby-Dick,* "Benito Cereno," "Bartleby," and "The Encantadas") as a prime example of Melville's finest work.

Based in part upon public and private records of the controversial *Somers* mutiny affair, in which (as previously noted) Melville's cousin Guert Gansevoort had been prominently involved,[3] the story details the tragic experience of a handsome and lovable but naive young sailor aboard the British warship *Indomitable* who, when falsely accused of conspiring mutiny by the innately evil master-at-arms, Claggart, impulsively strikes his accuser and kills him. This dire though unintended offense against naval discipline instantly requires a trial for murder, as the result of which the unfortunate hero — while openly pitied by the court-martial officers who recognize the perfect innocence of his motives — is condemned to death by hanging.

The chief responsibility for this decision rests with Captain Vere, a thoughtful and fatherly commander, who induces the other officers, and later Billy himself, to agree that the penalty imposed is the only one possible under the circumstances. Adherence to the strict letter of military law (in Melville's view, the Law of the World) — besides the possibility that Billy's transgression, if allowed to go unpunished, might set a dangerous example for other actual or potential mutineers — makes imperative the court's firm suppression of personal feelings and preferences in the case and a sentence demanded by the larger good of society and the British Navy.

Billy is hanged in a scene reminiscent of the Crucifixion, becoming, like Jesus, a willing sacrifice to social necessity. As in Milton's *Paradise Regained,* however, the climax of the story comes not at the passionate moment of the hero's martyrdom. Instead, it occurs when the actual choice is made between the two verdicts considered at the trial. The officers, tempted by conscience to declare Billy innocent — as a heavenly Judge might have done — find him guilty and condemn him. The crucial decision falls to Captain Vere; like Pilate, he is forced by necessity into a choice he abhors. In Milton's poem also, it will be recalled, the crisis occurs not at the passion but at the moment of choice. Christ, in Milton's interpretation, truly brings about the salvation of mankind when, in contrast with Adam, he decisively rejects the temptations of Satan, thereby setting the supreme example for humanity to follow and making it possible in His later sacrifice to offer an entirely pure soul to God.

In Billy one may see something of Melville himself as he was in 1848, a young hopeful of good intentions who — because of an innocent mistake which is the consequence of inexperience and a natural imperfection (in this case, his failure to appraise his American audience correctly) — is tried at the bar of public opinion and condemned without mercy. His *Mardi,* unintentionally shattering the intellectual peace by its violation of both social and literary rules and by its questioning of hallowed creeds and institutions, is recalled suggestively in Billy's involuntary blow of protest that fatally floors Claggart, the embodiment of evil. Yet *Billy Budd* should not be regarded primarily as a justification of Melville — "inner narrative" though he called it.

The spiritual message of the work is plainly of much wider application, and it fits with perfect logic into the whole fabric of Melville's thought. The story plainly says to the reader, at its deeper layers, that society may sometimes require the sacrifice of an individual member to preserve the accepted order and the general welfare, that such a state of affairs is not necessarily right but only unavoidably expedient at the present stage of human development, and that an intelligent person must bow to necessity without condoning it while feeling in his heart both admiration and pity for the sacrificial victim. Within the act of sacrifice, a symbol of expiation for the sins of all mankind, burns the spark of hope for eventual moral regeneration. With better understanding of himself, man may turn his man-of-war justice to absolute justice.

III *Assessment*

Billy Budd comes close to being Melville's "Everlasting Yea," though the affirmation is oblique, not positive. In *Mardi,* as has been noted, Melville considered and rejected various creeds, philosophies, and political and social theories in the search for truth; although he offered primitive Christianity as a social ideal and safe refuge for those willing to forego the quest of the absolute. *Moby-Dick,* while Promethean in certain respects, makes plain the folly of a stubborn defiance of man's fate. *Pierre* defines man's helplessness in the search for the meaning of true virtue and his inability to understand fully even himself. In *Clarel* the arguments for blind faith are tediously reviewed and one by one rejected, but the impression is conveyed that even in a state of weakness and ignorance there may be some hope. In *Billy Budd* the basis for idealism and hope is made more explicit.

Like *Moby-Dick, Billy Budd* can be read as merely an intensely interesting episode of maritime history. Its hero is not a cold abstraction or a personification but a living person, and his awkward speech impediment which occurs during moments of stress provides one of the proofs of his humanity. Claggart, evil as he is, possesses the necessary attributes of an earth creature; he rings true. Most carefully drawn of all the portraits in the book is that of Captain Vere. More thoughtful and high-minded than the usual commander of a warship, he typifies the well-educated English gentleman, worldly and brave — only perhaps a trifle thinner-blooded than most of his breed. Because of his known devotion to principle he receives from his brother officers the appelation of "Starry" Vere.

By making this noble captain the fulcrum upon which the plot is balanced, Melville proves that in *Billy Budd* he was concerned with far more than spinning a good yarn. The action hinges not upon the circumstances of Billy's crime nor upon his martyrdom, vital as these matters are. The factor of primary interest and moment — or, as noted, the climax of the plot (all other incidents and details occupy positions of secondary significance) — is Vere's decision in Billy's trial and his reasons for it. This revealing element in the structure of *Billy Budd* marks it as the work not of a purely emotional but of a thinking writer. Melville was less interested in the tragedy of Billy's hanging than in the principle behind it and its effect upon the participants — that is, all humanity. Vere makes his choice between the "chronological time" of absolute justice and the "horological time" of worldly necessity. He chooses the latter to achieve what he believes to be the larger good; yet he recognizes in Billy's condemnation a symbolical sacrifice: the victim suffers for and atones, Christ-like, for the sins of every man. Having presided at the ritual, Vere never fully recovers from the horror of having had such a decision forced upon him. He accepts, as Melville implies all human beings must, his responsibility as the agent of the sacrifice and as a partner in the definition of the crime, but he dies with Billy's name on his lips.

Billy Budd cannot justifiably be read as a document advocating direct social reform — in fact, except for its tragic view of the man-of-warishness of the world in general, it is not even a book against war. Some of Melville's earlier works contain arguments relating to specific social evils, but it would be a mistake to think of this aspect of his work as having major importance. Always more interested in metaphysics than in practical ethics or social theory, Melville probed the nature of individual man and his spiritual relationships — and not so much his relationships with other men as with the grand scheme of the universe. He examined internals rather than externals. True, he specifically condemned such abuses as naval flogging (at a time when many other voices were also being raised against it), but such matters were largely incidental to his main concerns. He rarely took a stand on political questions; but, like Emerson and Thoreau, he disavowed the patriotic fervor of "manifest destiny" that pushed the nation into the Mexican War and other similar acts of expansionism. In *Mardi,* although only in passing, he went so far as to caution his countrymen that the republican form of government requires careful judgment on the part of all citizens and that freedom wrongly employed can degenerate into mere license and mob rule. (To interpret his criticism of Jacksonian democracy and the thoughtless enthusiasm of the material-minded expansionists of his day as advocacy of socialism is, however, to ignore the total pattern of Melville's thought.)[4] He ab-

horred slavery but was not an abolitionist. He preached brotherhood and yet found mankind in the mass wrongheaded, corrupt,
and hardly worth saving.

Perhaps one of the reasons why Melville's most serious writings
failed in their purpose when they were first published was his un-
willingness to crusade for any cause but intellectual honesty. "Try
to get a living by the Truth — and go to the Soup Societies.
Heavens! Let any clergyman try to preach the Truth from its very
stronghold, the pulpit, and they would ride him out of his church
on his own pulpit bannister."⁵ Like Hawthorne, to whom the remarks above were addressed, Melville distrusted the social and
political movements that occupied (and still occupy) so large a
place in American life; he believed that the seeds of good and evil
are not inherent in a particular social organization or creed but lie
harbored in the human heart.⁶

So far as the controversy between religion and science is concerned, although it raged publicly throughout Europe and America
all during the nineteenth century, Melville took no strong stand on
one side or the other in his published works. He was aware, of
course, that numerous discoveries in geology, zoology, and the
other new sciences of the time had thrown serious doubt upon the
biblical story of creation and many other beliefs inherited from the
past and cherished as part of religious tradition. While fundamen-
talist churchmen — firmly relying upon every statement in both the
Old and the New Testament as literal truth — proclaimed the earth
to be (according to Hebrew chronology) something like six
thousand years old, busy scientists produced startling evidence of
life on earth going back not merely thousands but millions of years
into the past. Such evidence naturally raised questions regarding all
religious teaching; for if a single part of a reputedly infallible authority proves to be wrong, how can anyone believe the rest?

The problem of biblical authenticity, of so little interest in the
twentieth century, when religion and science have come to terms
and coexist peacefully, roused a painful upheaval in the minds of
thoughtful men a century ago. Most of them, like Evert Duyckinck, played safe by holding to what was conventional and generally ignoring the heresies of science. Others, like Hawthorne, escaped the agony of choice because they never fathomed the important role of science in modern thought. A few, like Melville's Margoth in *Clarel,* rudely thrust aside religion along with romanticism
and set about fashioning with ruthless efficiency a scientific image

of the world without God. To Melville this atheistic image looked like a cadaver, meticulously accurate in its details but wholly lacking warm breath and a pulsing heart. He could not help admiring science for its penetrating analysis and its practical accomplishments, but he sided with Carlyle in fearing it as a power that would mechanize human life and bewitch and entrap man with its computing skill just as the priesthood had bewitched and entrapped him with mystery.[7]

If Melville ever had any hope that science might one day supply the answers to the main spiritual questions of the universe, he ended by laying this hope aside. Science, he decided, dug with great skill into the complexities of life's outer mechanism, but it failed in its attempts to shed light on what makes the machinery run. For the solution of spiritual problems, thought must move on a spiritual plane. On the other hand, for Melville the religion of his time had abdicated its position of trust and was battling science for nothing more than the power to control men's mundane lives. The churches, camouflaged with false and useless dogma, doled out religion as a tranquilizer.

Melville's ultimate intellectual state may be described as a tentatively optimistic skepticism. He saw that man is capable of envisioning an ideal without achieving its realization. Though in a man-of-war society spiritual and ethical perfection remains unattainable, it is yet worthy of aspiration. Every thoughtful man's life constitutes a record of compromise between absolute good and worldly necessity. While resigned philosophically to the need for such a compromise, Melville could never admit, even in the mood of acceptance exhibited in *Billy Budd,* that the worldly "horologicals" — humanity's established standards of justice, truth, and virtue — are wholly right.

CHAPTER 9

Epilogue: The Melville Revival

I Aftermath

THE BRIEF obituary notices published in the New York City
newspapers and a few others after Melville's death in the
autumn of 1891 reveal not only the low estate of his literary reputation during that period but also the common lack of understanding
regarding the true nature of his work. A typical paragraph in the
New York *Daily Tribune* of September 29 summarized his career in
these words:

He won considerable fame as an author by the publication of a book in
1847 [*sic*] entitled "Type." . . . This was his best work, although he has
since written a number of other stories, which were published more for private than public circulation. . . . During the ten years subsequent to the
publication of this book he was employed at the New-York Custom
House.

The Press for the same date more or less correctly commented:

Of late years Mr. Melville — probably because he had ceased his literary
activity — has fallen into a literary decline, as the result of which his books
are now little known.
   Probably, if the truth were known, even his own generation has long
thought him dead, so quiet have been the later years of his life.

Some attempts to reestablish Melville's lost popularity had been
made by certain admiring readers even before his death, but with
only moderate success and with no encouragement at all from the
author himself. W. Clark Russell, to whom *John Marr* is dedicated,
had extolled his virtues as a writer of the sea in the 1880s and had
inscribed to Melville his maritime novel, *An Ocean Tragedy*

(1889).[1] Robert Buchanan in Great Britain had praised him in poetry, calling him "the one great imaginative writer fit to stand shoulder to shoulder with Whitman on that continent [America]."[2] A literary feature in the New York *Commercial Advertiser* in 1886 had brought attention to him as a "buried" author.[3] Robert Louis Stevenson had mentioned him enthusiastically in his letters from the South Seas printed in the New York *Sun;* to Stevenson, Melville was, in spite of lamentable misspellings of Polynesian names, the greatest of all South Seas writers.[4] Harper and Brothers had published an excerpt from *Moby-Dick* in a *Fifth Reader* issued in 1889, and in the same year H. S. Salt had written an appreciative essay on Melville for the *Scottish Art Review.*[5] With what now seems questionable taste in their selection of items, Stedman and Hutchinson had included "The Bell-Tower" and some of Melville's poems (together with a biographical sketch) in their comprehensive *Library of American Literature.*[6] All this does not obscure the fact that, at the time of his death, Melville actually was known to very few readers — and even to these chiefly as the author of *Typee* and *Omoo.* As he had feared, he was in danger of going down to posterity merely as "a man who had lived among the cannibals."[7]

During his lifetime, condensed and not strictly accurate biographies of Melville had appeared in such reference works as the Duyckinck brothers' widely read *Cyclopaedia of American Literature* (1855 and 1875) and the London publication, *Men of the Time* (1859). The first attempt at preparation of a more detailed biographical sketch occurred in 1891 when Melville's Pittsfield friend of long standing, the newspaper editor J. E. A. Smith, prepared an extensive obituary for the *Berkshire Evening Journal;* the material was afterwards published separately in an unprepossessing pamphlet of thirty pages. No book-length biography appeared, however, until Raymond M. Weaver began the vogue some three decades later.

II   *The Two Revivals*

Melville's death had the effect of setting off a mild flurry of interest in his neglected works. *Typee, Omoo, White-Jacket,* and *Moby-Dick* were all reissued within the following two years, and new appreciations of Melville's genius came from the pens of such critics and fellow craftsmen as Arthur Stedman,[8] R. H. Stoddard,[9] W. Clark Russell,[10] H. S. Salt,[11] Professor A. M. MacMechan,[12] and several others. This attention stimulated enough readership to encourage further publication of the early novels, particularly *Typee*. A measure of renewed acceptance may be said to have been achieved when the latter, along with *Omoo* and *Moby-Dick,* became permanent titles in the J. M. Dent and Company "Everyman's Library" series. The flurry died away rather quickly, having accomplished little for Melville except perhaps the resurrection of his fame as a writer of exciting narratives of maritime adventure. The deeper aspects of his art remained generally hidden until the second — and much more important — revival which took place about 1919, the centenary of his birth.

Numerous claims to priority have been put forth respecting the so-called "rediscovery" of Melville. It is clear that, while most critics and the public underrated or wholly ignored him, a small circle of perceptive readers — led by Wilbert Snow, Carl Van Doren, Frank J. Mather, and Viola Meynell, among others — formed a kind of advance guard in tacit preparation for the celebration of the Melville centennial. None took a more active part, however, than Raymond Weaver, who as a graduate student undertook to disinter what he had reason to suspect were the "mysteries" of Melville's life and surprisingly proliferous works. Given access by the great writer's descendants to family records — including the famous tin box containing the manuscripts of many poems and the unfinished *Billy Budd* — Weaver gathered enough interesting material to write and publish in 1921 a somewhat romanticized biography that almost immediately attracted the notice of American readers of the 1920s.

Weaver presented Melville as a misunderstood and suffering genius with a predilection toward mysticism who had fought a valiant but hopeless battle against the literary standards of his time, against society, and against his own melancholia. Though not entirely satisfactory as authentic biography, the book aroused other critics to explore Melville's works and ideas and thus inevitably to discover at last that he had been something more than a spinner of salty tales. Weaver subsequently edited for Constable and Company of London the only collected edition ever completed of Melville's known works — an edition enhanced by its inclusion of the first (albeit inaccurate) transcription of the spectacular *Billy Budd* manuscript.[13]

Following upon Weaver's heels, a host of other critics now seized upon Melville as a figure of unique interest and unexpected signifi-

cance in American literature. Satisfied with few facts about the
man himself, giving free play to sympathetic imagination, and
exploiting a recently acquired and rather sketchy knowledge of
popular Freudian psychology, they subjected nearly all his works to
delighted analysis, discovering there a prescience of amazing
power. Suddenly Melville became the center of clamorous discussion in what very nearly amounted to a cult.

More fruitful exploration of Melville's life and of his true place
in literature started in the 1930s, when literary scholars with patient
perseverance and scientific tools of research entered the field.[14]
Their work resulted in the gradual revision of many mistaken
theories (such as that of labeling Melville a mystic or that of blam-
ing all his troubles on a domineering mother) and the addition of
many essential details of his life. By 1945, the research had begun
to give a semblance of order to the chaos of discussion and theory
which had obscured the common reader's efforts to understand
Melville; in that year a group of American researchers organized a
society to further scientific investigation of Melville's life and
works, to exchange information regarding their own studies, and to
sponsor certain publishing projects. Among the members of this
organization have been most of the leading Melville scholars in the
United States, France, Germany, Austria, Japan, Australia, and
some South American and central European countries. By 1960, no
author in all American literature was being studied with more vigor
than was Melville.

III   Melville for the Modern Reader

For Melville to rise to his present prominence as a writer has
required an analytical age. Readers of the nineteenth century, filled
with romantic optimism and busily occupied in the ruthless
exploitation of a vast new continent, saw and enjoyed in his books
mainly a sensuous excitement of adventure in exotic surroundings.
This, in a romantic age, they could approve and appreciate. When
he veered in the direction of psychological realism and asked them
to think honestly about their motives and actions, they indignantly
deserted him. Americans today, having witnessed the disappear-
ance of the geographical frontier and having been shaken out of
isolation from the world's affairs through involvement in two
disastrous world wars, display greater willingness to examine
soberly the fundamental concepts of human life. Romantic opti-

mism has gradually given place to scientific objectivity and puzzled self-analysis. In a milieu in which readers urgently strive to know themselves, there has developed a very natural respect not only for Melville's acute powers of observation but also for his intellectual honesty. In many ways, his principal ethical and social ideas, though couched in the language of his own time, fit remarkably well into the intellectual currents of the twentieth century.

One should not, however, make the mistake of regarding Melville as essentially a philosopher. Though his philosophical ideas are both interesting and penetrating, he made no important original contributions in this field.[15] It is well to remember that, much as he read and speculated upon philosophical questions, his interest in the subject rested almost entirely upon his need for a trustworthy religious faith. As Hawthorne remarked in a passage already quoted, Melville was a man of deep religious feeling, "more fit for immortality than most of us." That he became, like Emerson, a comparative skeptic and in doing so shocked the staid conformists of his own generation (who regarded him, especially after *Pierre,* as morally dangerous) merely demonstrates his intellectual sincerity and betrays the stuffy shallowness of his critics. If he rejected the institutionalized creeds of his age and adopted an outlook mirroring the influence of science and approaching realism, he did so at the cost of severe emotional and mental anguish. He searched for truth with honesty and nobility, never once debasing his pursuit by seeking refuge in mysticism.

To be understood properly, Melville must be judged not as a philosopher or social critic but as a literary artist. The statement may seem at first thought absurdly obvious; yet the fact is often overlooked in many modern discussions of his works. His ideas, though they consistently entail philosophical speculation and social criticism, come to the reader not in the form of abstract and scientific dissertations; they come to him as literature. He wrote in his intense and passionate way about people — their actions, their aspirations, their inner thoughts, their feelings, their conflicts, and their personalities. He never learned Emerson's forte of attacking the problems of the universe with calm intellectuality and of discussing them in beautiful abstractions. "I stand for the heart," Melville asserted, thus declaring his intention of revealing not merely his mind but his whole spirit in his writing. He casts his brooding spell upon his reader less through the force of his intellect than through his feeling, less through his precise observation of detail than through his ability to invoke the response of inherent yearnings and emotions. One reads him because he succeeds in awakening within the reader, whether he describes delightful escapades in the Typee valley or the moral confusions of Pierre, the urging of every intelligent human being toward the full realization of individual identity through feeling.

Moby-Dick, now translated into all the important modern literary languages, will unquestionably remain for the foreseeable future the single book by which Melville will be best remembered. Better than any other work it reveals the magnificent scope of Melville's genius. Furthermore, it is now generally ranked as one of the great books of the world, "the one undisputed masterpiece of American literature." Like many another masterpiece, it is not light reading. The casual or superficial reader is almost certain to have trouble with it. The richest of its gold is imbedded in an immense deposit of ore that requires digging and smelting. Here and there huge diamonds glitter that may be picked up without much effort, but the book on the whole requires careful study. Where, then, lies its appeal?

To an extent, of course, the answer to this question depends upon the individual reader. Those who read the book simply for a vicarious experience of adventure at sea will be partially disappointed, for they will find the story full of digressions. Those who expect scientific realism will be distressed by its deliciously humorous treatment of the scientific facts of whales and whaling. Those who search through it for Melville's reasoned conclusions about religion and philosophy may set it aside mystified; for there are many questions but few answers. To appreciate the book fully, the reader must maintain an open mind; he must accept the book for what it is — not a straightforward narrative of adventure, not a treatise on the whaling industry, and not an allegorical commentary on the problems of man and fate, but an artfully unified combination of all three. The reader must be careful to avoid being misled by the profusion of symbols in the work. The opening sentence ("Call me Ishmael"), as a case in point, has thrown many an unwary reader off the track by giving him the impression that Melville's theme in the novel is loneliness and social outcasts. Whaling men, it is true, were often regarded as outcasts; and it is this idea that Melville intends to suggest, along with the narrator's reasons for going to sea on a whaler, and not a theme for the entire story.

No reader of *Moby-Dick* is likely to miss its powerful grandeur of expression and the pulsing heartbeat in its descriptions of men and nature. Cut these words, as Emerson declared of his favorite author, Montaigne, and they would bleed. However farfetched the principal outline of the plot and some of its details, however unmanageably the story fits the usual definitions of a typical novel, *Moby-Dick* holds its unique position in literature because it is instinct with the truth of life itself. In sweeping splendor it reveals the soul of man. It stirs the mind while it grips the emotions. Though it offers no clear answers, sets up no ideals of human behavior, and suggests no moral compromise, it raises in symbolic form nearly all the great metaphysical questions of man's intellectual and spiritual history and minutely examines them. In doing so, the book provides a description — unequaled for its emotional power — of the perennial human predicament. Like the life of man, the story has an end but no real conclusion. Ishmael, sole survivor of its tragic violence, still appears in the epilogue to be asking, "What does it all mean?"

If Melville had given in *Moby-Dick* the ready-made answers to the questions of human life and behavior that were given in other popular novels of his day, perhaps the book would have been more generally accepted; but it would hardly have been as great a work of literature. Instead of solving problems, it causes its reader to feel and think about them. In its own special way it constitutes for the reader a palpable experience — one involving the physical emotions, the mind, and the moral spirit. Thus reading it becomes, in a sense, very nearly an act of living.

Of Melville's other works, *Typee* and *Omoo* will no doubt long be read for their swift-moving narratives and for their youthful sense of wonder in the once-unspoiled paradise of the South Seas. *Mardi* will continue to attract readers interested in the highly imaginative and in social criticism and intellectual speculation presented as allegory. *Redburn* and *White-Jacket* will remain admirable as tales of young idealism's painful buffeting by the stern realities of life; the latter deserves particular attention for its artistic maturity and for certain signs that foreshadow *Moby-Dick*. *Pierre* seems likely to be read not so much for the story itself, striking as it is, as for its unusual probings into human psychology; readers must overlook its uneven quality and occasional ineptness for the brilliance of its theme and its honest facing up to moral realism. *Israel Potter* and *The Confidence-Man* probably have less to recommend them for survival than do Melville's other novels. They are both products of the author's period of decline and artistic frustration. Though competent in their handling of literary details, they lack the enthusiastic momentum of Melville at his best.

Among the shorter tales, "Bartleby," "Benito Cereno," and "The Encantadas," as has already been stated, appear most worthy of sustained popularity.[16] All deal in very different ways with man's reaction to evil. Together they comprise a trilogy of unusually beautiful and thrilling writing. In the first, the protagonist refuses to accept the present unsatisfactory state of the world and stubbornly asserts the supremacy of his individual nature by passive resistance — only to finish as a dead letter. In the second, the main character has been so thoroughly overwhelmed by the recognition of evil that he resigns all hope and retires in horror to die. In the third, the inevitable consequences of evil are implied in a series of somewhat varied sketches, but the nobility of mankind in suffering evil without complete loss of faith in ultimate good is very strongly suggested.

Melville's poetry, in spite of its many interesting aspects, can hardly lay claim to an enduring place in literature. As part of the Melville canon, it will be dissected and analyzed for traces of the author's opinions and feelings during the second half of his life. To the religious, philosophical, and social ideas of his mature years it clearly provides the key. Some of the poems, indeed, will be read with curiosity and even delight by readers of the future. The bulk of the poetry, however, seems destined to remain the preserve of scholars; they will continue to sift it for its ideas rather than for examples of literary excellence.

The one book likely to stand with *Moby-Dick* in the highest ranks of American literature is Melville's "inside narrative," *Billy Budd.* Though handicapped in the past by inaccuracies of transcription and editing, this brief novel has all the elements necessary for permanence: a noble and unified theme, a believable and lifelike plot, characters imbued with human feelings, inspired artistry in writing, and great compassion. Undergirding the story is Melville's persisting urge to discover the real truths behind human actions and motives. Though less wide-ranging in scope than its mighty predecessor, *Billy Budd* achieves an intensified literary effectiveness through its very compactness. With stunning brilliance it throws the pure beam of its lightning — if only for an instant — upon the warp and woof of human existence. Brief though it may be, its moment is a moment of conscience.

Melville's reputation as a leading American author is now secure.[17] His works are more and more widely read. The appreciation and understanding these works receive today was partially envisioned by Melville himself when he wrote in a letter to his British publisher Bentley on June 5, 1848, regarding the poor public reception of *Mardi:* "I have already received assurances that Mardi, in its higher purposes, has not been written in vain." We can say at last that nothing, indeed, of Melville's has been written in vain.

Notes and References

Chapter One

1. Melville's letters to Hawthorne were first printed by Julian Hawthorne in his *Nathaniel Hawthorne and His Wife*. All known letters of Melville have now been collected by Davis and Gilman. See Merrell R. Davis and William H. Gilman, eds., *The Letters of Herman Melville* (New Haven, 1960), p. 130.

2. Willard Thorp, ed., *Herman Melville: Representative Selections* (New York, 1938).

3. Published in *Timoleon* (1891).

4. One of the earliest interpretations is that by William S. Gleim in *The Meaning of Moby Dick* (New York, 1938). Several theories are discussed in Lorena M. Gary, " 'Rich Colors and Ominous Shadows,' " *South Atlantic Quarterly*, 37 (January, 1938), 41–45.

5. Melville's letter of January 8, 1952, *Letters*, p. 146.

6. Note their mutual interest in the story of Beatrice Cenci and similar examples.

7. *White-Jacket,* chap. 33.

8. *Moby-Dick,* chap. 42. Melville's chapter on whiteness has often been cited as a prime example of his use of symbols. It appears to be a kind of supplement to chapter 10 of François Rabelais's *Gargantua* and *Pantagruel,* in which Rabelais discusses whiteness as a symbol for joy and goodness. Melville shows that it may symbolize either good or evil.

9. *Moby-Dick,* chap. 36.

10. For further discussion of this theory, see Tyrus Hillway, "Melville's Art: One Aspect," *Modern Language Notes,* 62 (November, 1947), 477–80.

11. Charles R. Anderson, *Melville in the South Seas* (New York, 1939).

12. Howard P. Vincent, *The Trying-Out of Moby-Dick* (Boston, 1949).

13. Thorp, *Herman Melville,* pp. xlvii–xlviii.

14. See Russell Thomas, "Yarn for Melville's *Typee,*" *Philological Quarterly,* 15 (January, 1936), 16–29.

15. The count was made by the present writer while conducting research for his doctoral dissertation at Yale University. See Tyrus Hillway, *Melville and the Whale* (Stonington, Conn., 1950). Vincent also has information on the subject.

16. See chapter on *Moby-Dick* in D. H. Lawrence, *Studies in Classic American Literature* (New York, 1923).

17. Edward H. Rosenberry, *Melville and the Comic Spirit* (Cambridge, 1955).

18. See E. H. Eby, "Herman Melville's 'Tartarus of Maids,' " *Modern Language Quarterly,* 1 (March, 1940), 95–100.

19. See Merton M. Sealts, "Herman Melville's 'I and My Chimney,' " *American Literature,* 13 (May, 1941), 142–54.

20. See Tyrus Hillway, "Melville and the Young Revolutionaries," *Americana-Austriaca,* vol. 3, ed. Klaus Lanzinger (Vienna, 1974), pp. 43–58.

Chapter Two

1. Some time after Allan's death in 1832, the spelling of the name was changed by adding the final *e*, perhaps to make more obvious the family's connection with the aristocratic Scottish Melville clan.

2. Memorialized in "The Last Leaf" by Oliver Wendell Holmes.

3. Now on display in the Old State House at Boston.

4. October 11, 1828. This is the earliest letter of Melville for which we have the text.

5. Allan Melvill's letters are mainly in the Gansevoort-Lansing collection at the New York Public Library and in the Melville collection at Harvard's Houghton Library.

6. J. E. A. Smith, *The History of Pittsfield, Massachusetts, from the Year 1800 to the Year 1876* (Springfield, Mass., 1876), pp. 399–400.

7. For his perspicacious and thorough study of the evidence relating to Melville's life in Albany, modern Melville scholars are deeply indebted to William H. Gilman, whose *Melville's Early Life and Redburn* (New York, 1951) gives most of the essential details.

8. Gilman discovered from the official crew list of the *St. Lawrence* that Melville's name was mistakenly entered there as Norman instead of Herman.

9. What little is known about the reputed romance we owe to the indefatigable research of Gilman.

10. Raymond M. Weaver, Melville's first major biographer, accepted nearly all the information contained in Melville's first-person narratives as literally true. This impression was corrected by Charles R. Anderson in his pioneering study of Melville in the South Seas (see above). Traces of Melville's Pacific wanderings had been uncovered earlier by Robert S. Forsythe and others.

11. Melville called this tribe the Happars. His phonetic spelling of native Marquesan and Tahitian words, based as it was on his New York–New England pronunciation, differs in many respects from the accepted forms in use today.

12. For the best extended study of *Mardi* and its origins, see Merrell R. Davis, *Melville's Mardi: A Chartless Voyage* (New Haven, 1952).
13. Eleanor Melville Metcalf, ed., *Journal of a Visit to London and the Continent by Herman Melville, 1849–1850* (Cambridge, Mass., 1948).

Chapter Three

1. *Letters*, p. 109.
2. For a review of scholarship on this subject, see Vincent, *The Trying-Out of Moby Dick*.
3. James T. Fields, *Yesterdays with Authors* (Boston, 1872), 52–53.
4. Reported in [J. E. A. Smith], *Taghconic, the Romance and Beauty of the Hills*, by Godfrey Greylock (Boston, 1879), p. 318.
5. See Melville's poem, "Monody," written in memory of Hawthorne.
6. See Randall Stewart, "Hawthorne's Contributions to the *Salem Advertiser*," *American Literature*, 5 (January, 1934), 328–29.
7. For speculation on the revisions consult the introduction to the Mansfield-Vincent edition of *Moby-Dick* and Charles Olson, *Call Me Ishmael* (New York, 1947). In a prize-winning study, Barbour conjectures that Melville wrote *Moby-Dick* in three stages. See James Barbour, "The Composition of *Moby-Dick*," *American Literature*, 47 (November, 1975), 343–60. See also Robert Milder, "The Composition of *Moby-Dick:* A Review and a Prospect," *ESQ*, 23 (4th Quarter 1977), 203–216.
8. *Moby-Dick* was published in London in three volumes as *The Whale* on October 18.
9. See Tyrus Hillway, "Pierre, the Fool of Virtue," *American Literature*, 21 (May, 1949), 201–11.
10. "Melville's 'Agatha' Letter to Hawthorne," *New England Quarterly*, 2 (April, 1929), 296–307.
11. Scholars of the 1930s explained *Pierre* as a gesture of defiance against Melville's critics and as a blatant swan song. See, for example, E. L. Grant Watson, 'Melville's *Pierre*," *New England Quarterly*, 3 (April, 1930), 195–234. For a more modern view, compare Harrison Hayford, "The Significance of Melville's 'Agatha' Letters," *English Literary History*, 13 (December, 1946), 299–310.
12. *Letters*, p. 127.
13. Shepherd had recently published *Saratoga, a Tale of 1787.*
14. Howard C. Horsford, ed., *Melville's Journal of a Visit to Europe and the Levant, October 11, 1856–May 6, 1857* (Princeton, 1955).
15. A report of the visit is in Randall Stewart, *Nathaniel Hawthorne: A Biography* (New Haven, 1948), pp. 169–70.
16. The full name of the firm was Longman, Brown, Green, Longmans, and Roberts.

17. Melville's name is listed among future contributors on the back cover of early issues.
18. Author of *Nile Notes of a Howadji.*
19. A detailed account is given in Merton M. Sealts, Jr., *Melville as Lecturer* (Cambridge, Mass., 1957).
20. Lizzie Melville, in a letter to her mother in 1859, confided the surprising news: "Herman has taken to writing poetry. You need not tell anyone, for you know how such things get around."
21. Carl Bode, *The American Lyceum* (New York, 1956), p. 132.

Chapter Four

1. "The Scout toward Aldie" and other poems reveal Melville's personal familiarity with the scenes and incidents of warfare in Virginia.
2. See Walter D. Kring and Jonathan S. Carey, "Two Discoveries concerning Herman Melville," *Proceedings of the Massachusetts Historical Society,* 87 (1975), 137–41.
3. Probably the best extant likeness of Melville, the portrait has been given to Harvard University by Melville's descendants and is on display in the Houghton Library.
4. Intelligent British readers never lost faith, as did most Americans, in Melville's importance as a writer.
5. One of his poems, "The Admiral of the White" (a shorter version of "The Haglet"), appeared on May 17, 1885, in the *New York Daily Tribune* and the *Boston Herald.*
6. For a careful examination of the most important facts in the case, see Harrison Hayford, *The Somers Mutiny Affair* (Englewood Cliffs, N.J., 1959).
7. Several editions of *Billy Budd* have been published, Weaver's inaccurate version of 1924 being the first. F. Barron Freeman edited an elaborate edition with an introduction and notes in 1948 (Harvard University Press), but other scholars have disputed his readings of the manuscript and have suggested various changes. The definitive edition is *Billy Budd, Sailor,* ed. Harrison Hayford and Merton M. Sealts, Jr. (Chicago, 1962).

Chapter Five

1. Robert S. Forsythe, "Herman Melville in the Marquesas," *Philological Quarterly,* 15 (January, 1936), 1–15.
2. Printed July 1, 1846.
3. A judgment shared with Willard Thorp and most other Melville scholars.
4. James George Frazer, *The Belief in Immortality and Worship of the Dead* (London, 1913).
5. See Anderson, *Melville in the South Seas,* p. 190 and elsewhere. An

assessment of Melville's knowledge in various fields of science is made in Tyrus Hillway, "Melville's Education in Science," *Texas Studies in Language and Literature,* 16 (Fall, 1974), 411–25.

6. *Typee,* chap. 29.

7. Five editions of *Omoo* were published by Harper and Brothers during 1847.

8. Gilman, *Melville's Early Life and Redburn.*

9. Letter to Evert Duyckinck, December 14, 1849.

10. Letter to Richard Henry Dana, Jr., May 1, 1850.

11. Letter of Nathaniel Hawthorne to Evert Duyckinck, August 29, 1850 (Duyckinck Collection, New York Public Library).

Chapter Six

1. *Letters,* p. 128.

2. The names in *Mardi,* while ostensibly Polynesian, are actually drawn from the names of Persian characters and places in Herodotus and from Arabic words in Lane's translation of *The Arabian Nights.*

3. Melville discussed this idea in a letter to Hawthorne in March, 1851: "And perhaps, after all, there is *no* secret. We incline to think that the Problem of the Universe is like the Freemason's mighty secret, so terrible to all children. It turns out, at last, to consist in a triangle, a mallet, and an apron — nothing more!"

4. But see his letter of March 25, 1848, to John Murray, in which he says that "the reiterated imputation of being a romancer in disguise has at last pricked me into a resolution to show those who may take any interest in the matter, that a *real* romance of mine is no Typee or Omoo, & is made of different stuff altogether."

5. Judge Shaw, Melville's father-in-law, borrowed *Undine,* probably for Melville, from the Boston Athenaeum in March, 1847.

6. Leon Howard, *Herman Melville* (Berkeley, 1951), p. 114.

7. Thorp calls it (*Herman Melville*) "a slightly malicious smile," but I think he gives Melville credit for more sophistication than the latter actually possessed at this period of his career.

8. See his letters to Richard Bentley, the London publisher.

9. Merton M. Sealts, Jr., *Melville's Reading: A Check-List of Books Owned and Borrowed* (Madison, Milwaukee, and London, 1966), p. 48.

10. *Letters,* p. 109.

11. In bk. 1, chap. 11, "Prospectives."

12. Charles F. Richardson, *American Literature, 1607–1885,* 2 vols. (New York, 1887), II, 403–4.

13. See Olson, *Call Me Ishmael.* The most satisfactory analysis is that by Barbour in the article cited above (chap. 3, n. 7).

14. This problem is discussed in a recent German study: Hans Helmcke,

Die Funktion des Ich-Erzählers in Herman Melvilles Roman "Moby-Dick" (Munich, 1957). Available on microcards is Sister Marie of the Trinity Barry's "The Problem of Shifting Voice and Point of View in Melville's Early Novels and *Moby-Dick*," Diss., Catholic University of America, 1951.

15. See Gary, "Rich Colors and Ominous Shadows," and the Mansfield-Vincent edition of *Moby-Dick*.

16. *Letters*, pp. 124–25.

17. *Sartor Resartus*, bk. 2, chap. 7, "The Everlasting No." Melville's image of Ahab no doubt also owes much to Carlyle's *Heroes and Hero-Worship* and to Montaigne's essay, "How the Soul Dischargeth Her Passions upon False Objects When the True Fail It."

18. Lawrance Thompson, *Melville's Quarrel with God* (Princeton, N.J., 1952).

19. Thorp, *Herman Melville*, pp. lxxiii–lxxiv.

20. *Letters*, p. 142.

21. *Letters*, p. 125.

22. Stewart, "Hawthorne's Contributions," p. 170.

23. William Scoresby, Jr., *An Account of the Arctic Regions*, 2 vols. (Edinburgh, 1820), and Thomas Beale, *Natural History of the Sperm Whale* (London, 1839).

24. "The *Town-Ho's* Story" was published separately in *Harper's New Monthly* for October, 1851.

25. See James Dean Young, "The Nine Gams of the *Pequod*," *American Literature*, 25 (January, 1954), 449–63.

26. The Fields copy of *The Forester* is now in the possession of the author.

27. The Plinlimmon pamphlet reminds one of St. Paul's words in chapter 2 of the first letter to the Corinthians: "But the natural man [i.e., the nonenlightened or non-Christian] receiveth not the things of the Spirit of God: for they are foolishness unto him; neither can he know them, because they are spiritually discerned."

28. Arnold Bennett, in *The Savour of Life* (London, 1928), p. 249, says that in *Pierre* Melville "essays feats which the most advanced novelists of today imagine to be quite new."

Chapter Seven

1. *Letters*, p. 130.

2. See R. P. McCutcheon, "The Technique of Melville's *Israel Potter*," *South Atlantic Quarterly*, 27 (April, 1928), 167–74.

3. Richard Harter Fogle, *Melville's Shorter Tales* (Norman, Okla., 1960) and William B. Dillingham, *Melville's Short Fiction, 1853–1856* (Athens, Ga., 1977). See also Jay Leyda, ed., *The Complete Stories of Herman Melville* (New York, 1949).

4. Stanley T. Williams, " 'Follow Your Leader': — Melville's 'Benito Cereno', " *Virginia Quarterly Review,* 23 (Winter, 1947), 61–76. At a convivial dinner party one evening, an acquaintance of the present writer proposed the unusual hypothesis (to say the least!) that Melville intended "Benito Cereno" to be the means of inciting Southern slaves to revolt. "Follow Your Leader" was to be their rallying-cry.

5. See Newton Arvin, *Herman Melville* (New York, 1950), pp. 238–40; also F. O. Matthiessen, *American Renaissance* (New York, 1941), p. 508.

6. Rosalie Feltenstein, "Melville's 'Benito Cereno', " *American Literature,* 19 (November, 1947), 246.

7. Harold H. Scudder, "Melville's *Benito Cereno* and Captain Delano's *Voyages,*" *PMLA,* 42 (June, 1928), 502–32.

8. John J. Pullen, "Artemus Ward: The Man Who Made Lincoln Laugh," *Saturday Review,* Feb. 7, 1976, p. 20.

8. Quoted in Raymond M. Weaver, *Herman Melville: Mariner and Mystic* (New York, 1921), p. 360.

9. See Robert Penn Warren, "Melville the Poet," *Kenyon Review,* 8 (Spring, 1946), 208–23.

10. Editions of selected poems by Melville have been prepared by F. O. Matthiessen (1944), Hennig Cohen (1964), and Robert Penn Warren (1970).

11. Arvin, *Herman Melville,* p. 267.

12. Suggested by Professor Harry E. Hand, Air Force Institute of Technology.

13. Lewis Mumford, *Herman Melville* (New York, 1929), p. 299.

14. Edited by Walter E. Bezanson for Hendricks House.

15. Thorp, *Herman Melville,* lxxxix.

16. See Tyrus Hillway, "Melville and the Spirit of Science," *South Atlantic Quarterly,* 48 (January, 1949), 77–88.

17. Clarel's name is accented on the first syllable.

18. Mumford, *Herman Melville,* p. 322.

19. See Hugh W. Hetherington, *Melville's Reviewers* (Chapel Hill, 1961), p. 277.

20. The pool or stream of Siloam (or Siloah) in Jerusalem.

21. William Ellery Sedgwick, *Herman Melville: The Tragedy of Mind* (Cambridge, 1945), pp. 198–230.

Chapter Eight

1. See, for example, Sedgwick, *Herman Melville: The Tragedy of Mind.*

2. Much direct evidence of his overwhelming interest in metaphysics is recorded in Melville's 1849–1850 journal. See Metcalf, ed., *Journal of a Visit to London and The Continent.*

3. The details have been reviewed by Freeman in his edition of *Billy*

Budd, but see also Hayford's *The Somers Mutiny Affair.*
4. See article cited in note 20, chapter 1, above.
5. *Letters,* p. 127.
6. Note Melville's wholehearted praise of Hawthorne's fable, "Earth's Holocaust," in the famous review entitled "Hawthorne and His Mosses."
7. See the chapter on "Symbols" (bk. 3, chap. 3) in *Sartor Resartus.*

Chapter Nine

1. William Clark Russell, "Sea Stories," *Contemporary Review,* 46 (September, 1884), 343–63; and *In the Middle Watch* (New York, 1885).
2. Robert Buchanan, "Socrates in Camden," *The Academy,* 28 (August, 1885), 102–3. See also Buchanan's "Imperial Cockneydom," *Universal Review,* 4 (May–August, 1889), 71–91.
3. A report of Professor J. W. Henry Canoll's evening in the issue of January 18.
4. *In the South Seas* (London, 1888). For a more accessible edition, see *The Works of Robert Louis Stevenson* (New York, 1912), IX, 25–26.
5. H. S. Salt, "Herman Melville," *Scottish Art Review,* 2 (November, 1889), 186–90.
6. In Vol. VII of the eleven-volume *A Library of American Literature from the Earliest Settlement to the Present Time* (New York, 1889), eds. Edmund Clarence Stedman and Ellen Mackay Hutchinson.
7. See his letter to Nathaniel Hawthorne, June [1?], 1851.
8. See especially his "Melville of the Marquesas," *Review of Reviews,* 4 (November, 1891), 428–30.
9. New York *Mail and Express* for October 8, 1891, and elsewhere.
10. See Russell's "A Claim for American Literature," *North American,* 154 (February, 1892), 138–49.
11. See Salt's "Marquesan Melville," *Gentleman's Magazine,* NS 48 (March, 1892), 248–57.
12. Archibald MacMechan, "The Best Sea Story Ever Written," *Queen's Quarterly,* 7 (1899), 120–30.
13. Published in sixteen volumes, 1922–24. See Bibliography.
14. Hugh W. Hetherington completed the first doctoral dissertation on Melville at the University of Michigan in 1933.
15. See Ralph Henry Gabriel, *The Course of American Democratic Thought* (New York, 1956), pp. 70–79.
16. These have recently been republished by Harper and Brothers as *Three Shorter Novels of Herman Melville* (1962).
17. See *The Recognition of Herman Melville,* ed. Hershel Parker (Ann Arbor, Mich., 1967).

Selected Bibliography

PRIMARY SOURCES

1. Collected Editions

The Writings of Herman Melville. Harrison Hayford, Hershel Parker, and G. Thomas Tanselle, general editors. Evanston: Northwestern University Press and Newberry Library, 1968–. When completed, will provide an authoritative text of all Melville's writings, with extensive historical and textual notes. The following titles have been published: *Typee, Omoo, Mardi, Redburn, White-Jacket, Pierre.*

Complete Works of Herman Melville. Howard P. Vincent, general editor. Chicago: Hendricks House, 1947–. An incomplete edition, announced in 1946 but now apparently abandoned. Volumes published to 1969 were prepared by various editors and are uneven in quality. They include *Collected Poems, Piazza Tales, Pierre, Moby-Dick, The Confidence Man, Clarel, Omoo. Clarel,* edited with copious notes by Walter E. Bezanson (1960), is the best published edition of the poem to date.

The Works of Herman Melville. Standard Edition. 16 vols. London: Constable, 1922–1924; rpt. New York: Russell & Russell, 1963. The only collected edition containing the bulk of Melville's writings, but based largely on British versions of the text. The last four volumes were published in 1924 as supplements; they contain poetry, sketches, and the first appearance in print of *Billy Budd* as transcribed (rather inaccurately) and edited by Raymond Weaver.

Romances of Herman Melville. New York: Tudor Publishing Company, 1931. One-volume collection containing seven of Melville's novels.

2. First Editions

Narrative of a Four Months' Residence among the Natives of a Valley of the Marquesas Islands. Issued in two parts in Murray's Home and Colonial Library. London: John Murray, 1846. "The Story of Toby" published separately the same year and later added to the book as an appendix.

Typee: A Peep at Polynesian Life. New York: Wiley and Putnam, 1846. Revised edition, including "The Story of Toby," published in 1847.

163

Omoo: A Narrative of Adventures in the South Seas. London: John Murray, 1847; New York: Harper and Brothers, 1847.

Mardi: and a Voyage Thither. 3 vols. London: Richard Bentley, 1849; 2 vols. New York: Harper and Brothers, 1849.

Redburn: His First Voyage. London: Richard Bentley, 1849; New York: Harper and Brothers, 1849.

White-Jacket; or The World in a Man-of-War. London: Richard Bentley, 1850; New York: Harper and Brothers, 1850.

The Whale, 3 vols. London: Richard Bentley, 1851.

Moby-Dick; or, The Whale. New York: Harper and Brothers, 1851.

Pierre; or the Ambiguities. New York: Harper and Brothers, 1852; London: Sampson, Low, Son, and Company, 1852.

Israel Potter: His Fifty Years of Exile. New York: G. P. Putnam and Company, 1855; London: G. Routledge and Company, 1855.

The Piazza Tales. New York: Dix and Edwards, 1856; London: Sampson, Low, Son, and Company, 1856.

The Confidence-Man: His Masquerade. New York: Dix, Edwards and Company, 1857. London: Longman, Brown, Green, Longmans, and Roberts, 1857.

Battle-Pieces, and Aspects of the War. New York: Harper and Brothers, 1866.

Clarel: A Poem and Pilgrimage in the Holy Land. New York: G. P. Putnam's Sons, 1876.

John Marr and Other Sailors. New York: De Vinne Press, 1888.

Timoleon. New York: Caxton Press, 1891.

Billy Budd, Foretopman. Ed. Raymond Weaver. In *Billy Budd and Other Prose Pieces.* London: Constable and Company, 1924.

3. Letters and Journals

"Journal of Melville's Voyage in a Clipper Ship." *New England Quarterly,* 2 (January, 1929), 120–39.

Family Correspondence of Herman Melville, 1830–1904. Ed. Victor H. Paltsits. New York: New York Public Library, 1929.

Journal of a Visit to London and the Continent by Herman Melville, 1849–1850. Ed. Eleanor Melville Metcalf. Cambridge: Harvard University Press, 1948.

Melville's Journal of a Visit to Europe and the Levant, October 11, 1856–May 6, 1857. Ed. Howard C. Horsford. Princeton: Princeton University Press, 1955.

The Letters of Herman Melville. Ed. Merrell R. Davis and William H. Gilman. New Haven: Yale University Press, 1960.

4. Representative Modern Editions

The Apple-Tree Table and Other Sketches. Ed. Henry Chapin. Princeton: Princeton University Press, 1922.

Battle-Pieces and Aspects of the War. Ed. Sidney Kaplan. Amherst: University of Massachusetts Press, 1972.
The Battle-Pieces of Herman Melville. Ed. Hennig Cohen. New York: Thomas Yoseloff, 1963.
Billy Budd and Other Tales. Afterword by Willard Thorp. Signet Classics. New York: New American Library, 1961.
Billy Budd, Sailor. Ed. Harrison Hayford and Merton M. Sealts, Jr. Chicago: University of Chicago Press, 1962. The definitive edition, based upon thorough study of the original manuscript, with excellent introduction and notes.
Complete Stories of Herman Melville. Ed. Jay Leyda. New York: Random House, 1949. Well-edited collection of Melville's tales and sketches, with biographical introduction and notes.
The Confidence Man. Ed. Hershel Parker. New York: W. W. Norton, 1971. Critical Editions series.
The Confidence Man: His Masquerade. Ed. H. Bruce Franklin. Indianapolis: Bobbs-Merrill, 1967.
The Confidence-Man: His Masquerade. New York: Grove Press, 1955.
Great Short Works of Herman Melville. Ed. Warner Berthoff. New York: Harper and Row, 1970.
Herman Melville: Representative Selections. Ed. Willard Thorp. New York: American Book Company, 1938. Important for its excellent introductory essay, though now somewhat out of date.
His Fifty Years of Exile (Israel Potter). Intro. Lewis Leary, New York: Sagamore Press, 1957. American Century series.
Israel Potter: His Fifty Years of Exile. New York: Warner, 1974.
John Marr and Other Sailors. Folcroft, Pa.: Folcroft Press, 1974.
Mardi. New Haven: College & University Press, 1973. Masterworks of Literature series. Modernized punctuation and spelling.
Moby-Dick, or the Whale. Ed. Harrison Hayford and Hershel Parker. New York: W. W. Norton, 1976. Critical Editions series.
Moby Dick, or, The Whale. Ed. Charles Feidelson, Jr. Indianapolis: Bobbs-Merrill, 1964.
Moby Dick, or, The Whale. Intro. Leon Howard. New York: Random House, 1950. Modern Library edition.
Moby-Dick, or, The Whale. Boston: Houghton Mifflin, 1956. Riverside Editions series.
Omoo, A Narrative of Adventures in the South Seas. New York: Grove Press, 1958.
Pierre, or, The Ambiguities. Preface by H. M. Tomlinson and introduction by John Brooks Moore. New York: E.P. Dutton, 1929.
Pierre, or The Ambiguities. Ed. Robert S. Forsythe. New York: Alfred A. Knopf, 1930. Still one of the best modern editions.
Pierre, or, The Ambiguities. New York: Grove Press, 1957.

Poems of Herman Melville. Ed. Douglas Robillard. New Haven: College & University Press, 1976.

The Portable Melville. Ed. Jay Leyda. New York: Penguin, 1976.

Redburn: His First Voyage. Garden City, N.Y.: Doubleday, 1957. Anchor Books.

Selected Poems of Herman Melville. Ed. Hennig Cohen. Carbondale: Southern Illinois University Press, 1964.

Selected Poems of Herman Melville. Ed. Robert Penn Warren. New York: Random House, 1970.

Selected Tales and Poems. New York: Holt, Rinehart and Winston, 1950. Rinehart Editions series.

Timoleon. Folcroft, Pa.: Folcroft, 1976.

Typee. Ed. George Woodcock. New York: Penguin, 1972.

Typee: A Real Romance of the South Seas. Intro. by C. Merton Babcock. New York: Harper and Row, 1959. Harper's Modern Classics.

Typee and Billy Budd. Ed. Milton R. Stern. New York: E. P. Dutton, 1958.

White-Jacket, or The World in a Man-of-War. Intro. by William Plomer. New York: Grove Press, 1956.

White-Jacket; Or, the World in a Man-of-War. Ed. Arthur Humphreys. New York: Oxford University Press, 1966.

SECONDARY SOURCES

1. Biography

ANDERSON, CHARLES ROBERTS. *Melville in the South Seas.* New York: Columbia University Press, 1939; rpt. New York: Dover Press, 1966. This first detailed study of Melville's life as a sailor in the Pacific provides an accurate, nearly day-to-day account of the adventures on which *Typee, Omoo, White-Jacket,* and parts of *Moby-Dick* are based.

ARVIN, NEWTON. *Herman Meville.* New York: William Sloane Associates, 1950. Interpretation of Melville's life and works in psychological terms. Beautifully written but not wholly trustworthy in details.

DAVIS, MERRELL R. *Melville's Mardi: A Chartless Voyage.* New Haven: Yale University Press, 1952. Relates the details of Melville's life from 1844 to 1847 and examines the origins and meaning of *Mardi.*

FREEMAN, JOHN. *Herman Melville.* English Men of Letters Series. London: Macmillan, 1926. A short biography based largely on materials from Weaver and other authors, with some original comment and criticism.

GILMAN, WILLIAM H. *Melville's Early Life and Redburn.* New York: New York University Press, 1951. By revealing hitherto undiscovered facts of Melville's youth, shows that Melville's novels cannot be relied on as autobiography. Thoroughly examines *Redburn* as a work of art.

HOWARD, LEON. *Herman Melville: A Biography.* Berkeley: University of California Press, 1951. A sensible biography reviewing everything known about Melville's life and career.

LEYDA, JAY. *The Melville Log: A Documentary Life of Herman Melville, 1819–1891.* 2 vols. New York: Harcourt, Brace, 1951; rpt. with additions, New York: Gordian, 1969. A monumental collection of documents and references that recreate Melville's life and activities year by year. Indispensable for the Melville scholar.

METCALF, ELEANOR MELVILLE. *Herman Melville: Cycle and Epicycle.* Cambridge: Harvard University Press, 1953. A biography by Melville's granddaughter, with family reminiscences.

MILLER, EDWIN HAVILAND. *Melville.* New York: George Braziller, 1975. Presents Melville unconvincingly as a sexual deviate in love with Hawthorne.

MUMFORD, LEWIS. *Herman Melville.* New York: Harcourt, Brace, 1929, rev. 1962. A biography which attempts an analysis of Melville's mind. Errs by accepting much of Melville's writing as autobiographical.

SEALTS, MERTON M., JR. *The Early Lives of Melville.* Madison: University of Wisconsin Press, 1974. Excellent collection of nineteenth-century biographical sketches.

SMITH, J. E. A. *Herman Melville,* written for the *Evening Journal.* Pittsfield, Massachusetts, 1891. Early biographical sketch.

STONE, GEOFFREY. *Melville.* New York: Sheed and Ward, 1949. Has a slight Roman Catholic bias.

WEAVER, RAYMOND M. *Herman Melville: Mariner and Mystic.* New York: George H. Doran, 1921. The first full-length biography. Important but now outdated.

2. Criticism

AUDEN, W. H. *The Enchafed Flood.* New York: Random House, 1950. "Romantic iconography of the sea." Includes much on Melville.

BAIRD, JAMES R. *Ishmael.* Baltimore: Johns Hopkins University Press, 1956. Primitivism and symbolism in literature.

BERNSTEIN, JOHN. *Pacifism and Rebellion in the Writings of Herman Melville.* The Hague: Mouton, 1964. Unconvincing attempt to show that Melville changed his attitude from pacifism to rebellion against society.

BERTHOFF, WARNER. *The Example of Melville.* Princeton: Princeton University Press, 1962. Detailed consideration of Melville as literary craftsman.

BICKLEY, R. BRUCE, JR. *The Method of Melville's Short Fiction.* Durham: Duke University Press, 1975.

BORTON, JOHN. *Herman Melville: The Philosophical Implications of Literary Technique in Moby-Dick.* Amherst, Mass.: Amherst College Press, 1961.

BOWEN, MERLIN. *The Long Encounter: Self and Experience in the Writings of Herman Melville*. Chicago: University of Chicago Press, 1960. Melville's concept of self and its effect upon his choice of subject, imagery, view of character, narrative structure, and attitude toward his material.

BRASWELL, WILLIAM. *Melville's Religious Thought*. Durham: Duke University Press, 1943; rpt. New York: Pageant Book Company, 1959. Shows Melville's hesitancy between religious belief and disbelief.

BREDAHL, A. CARL, JR. *Melville's Angles of Vision*. Gainesville: University of Florida Press, 1972. The function of perspective in Melville's literary art.

BROWNE, RAY B. *Melville's Drive to Humanism*. Lafayette, Ind.: Purdue University Studies, 1971. Discussion of Melville's concern for the "common man."

CHASE, RICHARD, ed. *Melville: A Collection of Critical Essays*. Englewood Cliffs, N.J.: Prentice-Hall, 1962. Critical essays on Melville by various authors.

DILLINGHAM, WILLIAM B. *An Artist in the Rigging*. Athens: University of Georgia Press, 1972. Impressionistic discussion of themes in Melville's early novels.

_____. *Melville's Short Fiction, 1853–1856*. Athens: University of Georgia Press, 1977.

FEIDELSON, CHARLES, JR. *Symbolism and American Literature*. Chicago: University of Chicago Press, 1953. Symbolism in the works of Hawthorne, Whitman, Melville, and Poe.

FINKELSTEIN, DOROTHEE METLITSKY. *Melville's Orienda*. New Haven: Yale University Press, 1961. Melville's use of sources relating to the Middle and Far East.

FOGLE, RICHARD HARTER. *Melville's Shorter Tales*. Norman, Okla.: University of Oklahoma Press, 1960. Describes and analyzes fifteen of Melville's tales and sketches.

FRANKLIN, H. BRUCE. *The Wake of the Gods: Melville's Mythology*. Stanford, Calif.: Stanford University Press, 1963. Discussion of Melville's uses of myth and mythology in some of his works. Some unsupported opinion and politically slanted interpretations.

FRIEDRICH, GERHARD. *In Pursuit of Moby Dick*. Wallingford, Pa.: Pendle Hill, 1958. Deals with Melville's image of man.

GLEIM, WILLIAM S. *The Meaning of Moby Dick*. New York: Brick Row Book Shop, 1938. Elaborate attempt at allegorical interpretation.

HAYFORD, HARRISON, ed. *The Somers Mutiny Affair*. Englewood Cliffs, N.J.: Prentice-Hall, 1959. Gives the story of the famous mutiny and its effect on public opinion. Important as background for *Billy Budd*.

HERBERT, T. WALTER. *Moby-Dick and Calvinism*. New Brunswick, N.J.: Rutgers University Press, 1977. Shows how Melville's novel reflects the disintegration of nineteenth-century religious views.

HETHERINGTON, HUGH W. *Melville's Reviewers: British and American, 1846–1891.* Chapel Hill: University of North Carolina Press, 1961. The critical reception of Melville's works during his lifetime.

HILLWAY, TYRUS. *Melville and the Whale.* Stonington, Conn.: Stonington Publishing Company, 1950; rpt. Folcroft, Pa.: Folcroft Press, 1969. Analyzes Melville's knowledge of cetology and use of cetological sources.

———, and LUTHER S. MANSFIELD, eds. *Moby-Dick Centennial Essays.* Dallas: Southern Methodist University Press, 1953. Contains nine papers delivered by prominent Melville scholars at centennial celebrations held during 1951.

HOWARD, LEON. *Herman Melville.* Minneapolis: University of Minnesota Press, 1961. Short pamphlet on Melville's life and works.

JAMES, C. L. R. *Mariners, Renegades, and Castaways.* New York: James, 1953. Propagandistic discussion of social and political implications in Melville's works.

KENNY, VINCENT. *Herman Melville's Clarel: A Spiritual Autobiography.* Hamden, Conn.: Archon Books, 1973. Defines Melville's religious ideas as essentially agnostic.

LEBOWITZ, ALAN. *Progress into Silence: A Study of Melville's Heroes.* Bloomington: Indiana University Press, 1970. Attempts to trace the development of Melville's psychobiography.

LEVIN, HARRY. *The Power of Blackness.* New York: Alfred A. Knopf, 1958. Sees the favorite themes of Hawthorne, Poe, and Melville as rooted in the Puritan ethic and the Transcendentalist world view.

MASON, RONALD. *The Spirit above the Dust: A Study of Herman Melville.* London: John Lehmann, 1951. Critical discussions of Melville's life and works.

MILLER, JAMES E., JR. *A Reader's Guide to Herman Melville.* New York: Farrar, Straus and Cudahy, 1962. Short introduction to Melville and his works. Says Melville favored "compromise with his ideals . . . in order to come to terms with the world's evil."

MILLER, PERRY. *The Raven and the Whale.* New York: Harcourt, Brace and Company, 1956. Describes the literary atmosphere in America during the early years of Melville's career.

OLSON, CHARLES. *Call Me Ishmael.* New York: Harcourt, Brace, 1947; rpt. New York: Grove Press, 1958. Highly individualistic discussion of Melville's mentality, the influence of Shakespeare, and the writing of *Moby-Dick.*

PARKER, HERSHEL, ed. *The Recognition of Herman Melville.* Ann Arbor: University of Michigan Press, 1967. New information on the development of Melville's reputation.

PERCIVAL, M. O. *A Reading of Moby Dick.* Chicago: Univresity of Chicago Press, 1950. Helpful study guide.

POMMER, HENRY F. *Milton and Melville.* Pittsburgh: University of Pittsburgh Press, 1950. Influence of Milton on Melville's ideas and symbols.

ROSENBERRY, EDWARD H. *Melville and the Comic Spirit.* Cambridge: Harvard University Press, 1955. Revealing study of Melville as humorist.

SEALTS, MERTON M., JR., comp. *Melville's Reading: A Check List of Books Owned and Borrowed.* Madison: University of Wisconsin Press, 1966. A list of books known to have been read or purchased by Melville, many having provided materials for his own works.

_____. *Melville as Lecturer.* Cambridge: Harvard University Press, 1957. Thorough study of Melville's brief career as lecturer, with reconstruction of the lectures themselves from newspaper accounts.

SEDGWICK, WILLIAM ELLERY. *Herman Melville, The Tragedy of Mind.* Cambridge: Harvard University Press, 1945. Interesting early interpretation of Melville's career as a tragic search for truth.

SELYE, JOHN. *Melville: The Ironic Diagram.* Evanston: Northwestern University Press, 1970. Discusses Melville's unfulfilled search for truth and fixed moral standards.

STAFFORD, WILLIAM T., ed. *Melville's Billy Budd and the Critics.* San Francisco: Wadsworth Publishing Company, 1961. Reprints *Billy Budd* from Freeman's corrected text, with examples of critical comments on the work.

STANONIK, JANEZ. *Moby-Dick: The Myth and the Symbol.* Ljubljana, Yugoslavia: Ljubljana University Press, 1962. A study of sailors' yarns, folk tales, and other traditions regarding white whales.

STEIN, WILLIAM BYSSHE. *The Poetry of Melville's Last Years.* Albany: State University of New York Press, 1970. Analyzes and explicates Melville's poems after *Clarel.*

STERN, MILTON R. *The Fine Hammered Steel of Herman Melville.* Urbana: University of Illinois Press, 1957. Identifies Melville's main philosophical theme as cosmic and antiidealistic "naturalism."

_____, ed. *Discussions of Moby-Dick.* Boston: D.C. Heath, 1960. A collection of critical comments.

THOMPSON, LAWRANCE. *Melville's Quarrel with God.* Princeton: Princeton University Press, 1952. Argues that Melville hated God for introducing evil into man's life.

VINCENT, HOWARD P. *The Trying-Out of Moby-Dick.* Boston: Houghton Mifflin, 1949. Discusses the background of *Moby-Dick* and its literary sources.

_____. *The Tailoring of Melville's White-Jacket.* Evanston: Northwestern University Press, 1970. A study of sources used in the writing of *White-Jacket.*

_____, ed. *Melville Annual 1965: A Symposium.* Kent: Kent State University Press, 1966. A collection of papers dealing with "Bartleby the Scrivener."

———, eds. *Melville and Hawthorne in the Berkshires: A Symposium.* Kent: Kent State University Press, 1968. A collection of papers delivered at a Melville Society conference in the Berkshire Hills area.

WALKER, FRANKLIN. *Irreverent Pilgrims.* Seattle: Univresity of Washington Press, 1974. The reports of Melville, J. Ross Browne, and Mark Twain on their visits to the Holy Land.

WOODRESS, JAMES, ed. *Eight American Authors.* New York: Norton, 1971. Reviews important research and criticism regarding the most important American writers, with a chapter on Melville.

WRIGHT, NATHALIA. *Melville's Use of the Bible.* Durham: Duke University Press, 1949. Shows that the Bible was one of Melville's chief sources for symbols, language, and ideas.

ZOELLNER, ROBERT. *The Salt-Sea Mastodon.* Berkeley: University of California Press, 1973. Interprets *Moby-Dick* as essentially an expression of Ishmael's views and sees him as the real hero of the work.

Index

Names of characters and places in Melville's works are followed by the title — in parenthesis — of the work in which they appear.

Acushnet, 35, 36, 37, 69
"After the Pleasure Party," 127
"Agatha" story, 49, 50
Ahab, Captain (*Moby-Dick*), 22, 35, 85–86, 88–93, 95–98, 103–106, 116
Albany, (N.Y.), *M's* life in, 29–32
Albany Academy, 30, 34, 59
Albany Classical School, 32
Albany Female Academy, 31
Albany Microscope, 32
Albany Young Men's Association, 32
Albatross, 99, 101
Allen, Ethan, 114–15
All Souls Unitarian Church, 62
Ames, Nathaniel, 74
Anatomy of Melancholy, 81
Anderson, Charles B., 23
"Apple-Tree Table, The," 53
Aranda, Don Alexandro ("Benito Cereno"), 118
Arcturus magazine, 41
Arrowhead, 46, 47, 52, 53, 58, 59
"Art" (quoted), 19–20
Atlantic Monthly, 56
Atufal ("Benito Cereno"), 117
Authorship, *M's* choice of, 18–19

Babbalanja (*Mardi*), 78, 79
Babo ("Benito Cereno"), 117, 118
Bachelor, 102
Bachelor's Delight, 116
"Bartleby the Scrivener," 50, 115–16, 136, 139, 152
Battle-Pieces and Aspects of the War, 61, 124, 126, 127, 128, 131, 138
Beale, Thomas, 23, 97, 128
"Bell-Tower, The," 52, 115, 146
"Benito Cereno," 25, 51–52, 115,

116–18, 136, 139, 152
Bentley, Richard (London publisher), 43, 44, 48, 83, 153
Berkshire Eagle, 59
Berkshire Evening Journal, 146
Bildad, Captain (*Moby-Dick*), 95
Billy Budd, Sailor, 20, 39, 67, 75, 138–44, 147, 152
Blackwood's Magazine, 109
Bland (*White-Jacket*), 75
Bolton, Harry (*Redburn*), 73–74
Bon Homme Richard, 115
Book of Nature, 128
"Bridegroom Dick," 127
Broadhall, 45
Brown, Captain Oliver, 33
Browne, Sir Thomas, 81
Brunswick (N.Y.), *M* teaches school at, 34
Buchanan, Robert, 66, 146
Budd, Billy, (*Billy Budd, Sailor*), 139–40
Buffalo Commercial Advertiser, 68
Burton, Robert, 81
Byron, Lord, 131

Carlyle, Thomas, 27, 45, 83–86, 108, 128, 144
Century Club, 65
Cereno, Benito ("Benito Cereno"), 117–18
Cetology, 87, 97
Chambers, Robert, 128
Charles and Henry, 38, 41, 72
Chase, Jack (*White-Jacket*), 39, 75
"Chattanooga," 61, 126
"Chronometricals and Horologicals," 110

172

Claggart (*Billy Budd, Sailor*), 75, 139, 140, 141
Clarel, 56, 64, 65, 128–34, 138, 141, 143
Clarel (*Clarel*), 129, 134
Claret, Captain (*White-Jacket*), 75
"Cock-a-Doodle-Doo!'', 50
Confidence-Man, The, 19, 25, 35, 51, 53, 54, 55, 56, 75, 119–21, 128, 136, 138, 151; publication of, 56
Constable and Company, 147
"Cumberland, The,'' 61, 126
Curtis, George William, 57
Customs, *M* as inspector of, 62, 64
Cuticle, Dr. (*White-Jacket*), 76
Cyclopedia of American Literature, 146

Daggoo (*Moby-Dick*), 91, 97, 99
Dana, Richard Henry, Jr., 46, 56, 72, 87
Dante, 79, 80, 81, 132
Darwin, Charles, 26
Darwinism, 84, 100, 101
Delano, Amasa, 51–52, 116–18
Delight, 102–103
Democratic Press and Lansingburgh Advertiser, 33
Dent, J. M. & Company, 147
Derwent (*Clarel*), 129, 132
Divine Comedy, The, 79, 81
Dix and Edwards, 54, 56
Dolly, 69
Dominora (*Mardi*), 79
"Donelson,'' 127
Duyckinck, Evert, 41, 45, 47, 48–49, 54, 65, 69, 146
Duyckinck, George, 47, 56, 146

Eaton, Joseph, 63
Eimeo (*Omoo*), 37
Elijah (*Moby-Dick*), 96
Ellis, William, 70, 128
Emerson, Ralph Waldo, 26, 142, 149, 151
"Encantadas or Enchanted Islands, The,'' 50, 115, 118–19, 139, 152
Enceladus (*Pierre*), 110, 112
Erie Canal, 33
Essex, 119
"Ethan Brand,'' 91

Faerie Queene, The, 81

Fairhaven (Mass.), *M* sails from, 35
Fanning, Nathaniel, 114
"Fast-Fish and Loose-Fish'' passage in *Moby-Dick* (quoted), 25
Father Mapple (*Moby-Dick*), 95, 100
Fayaway (*Typee*), 37, 69
Fedallah (*Moby-Dick*), 86, 92, 105
Feltenstein, Rosalie, 118
"Fiddler, The,'' 51
Fidèle, 75, 119
Field, David Dudley, 45
Fields, James T., 45, 109
Fifth Reader (Harper and Bros.), 146
Flask (*Moby-Dick*), 97
Fleece (*Moby-Dick*), 100
Flogging, *M's* criticism of, 76
Fly, Eli, 34, 35
Fly, Harriet, 34
Fogle, Richard, 115
Foresters, The, 109
"Fragments from a Writing Desk,'' 33, 68
Franklin, Benjamin, 114

Gabriel (*Moby-Dick*), 101
Galapagos Islands, 35, 49, 118–119
Galena (Ill.), *M* visits, 34–35
Gansevoort, (Lieutenant) Guert, 39, 139
Gansevoort, (General) Peter (*M's* grandfather), 29
Gansevoort, Peter *(M's* uncle), 31, 33, 64, 65
Gargantua and Pantagruel, 81
"'Gees,' The,'' 53
"Gettysburg,'' 61, 126
Gilman, William, 73
Glendinning, Mrs. (*Pierre*), 107
"Gold Bug, The,'' 117
Good, John Mason, 128
Grant, Ulysses S., 60
"Grass,'' 127
Greenbush (N.Y.), *M* teaches school at, 34
Greene, Richard Tobias ("Toby''), 36, 37, 68–69
Greylock, Mount, 46, 47

Happa tribe ("Happars''), 36
"Happy Failure, The,'' 51
Hardy, Thomas, 122
Harper and Brothers, 47, 48, 49, 51, 53,

60, 61, 118, 146
Harper's Magazine, 50, 51, 53, 61
Hautia (*Mardi*), 79, 80, 81
Hawthorne, Nathaniel, 18, 21, 26, 45,
    46, 47, 48, 49, 50, 55, 56, 77, 78, 86,
    89, 91, 92, 93, 109, 113, 119, 143,
    144, 149
Hawthorne, Sophia (Mrs. Nathaniel),
    21, 48, 55, 108
Heroes and Hero-Worship, 45
Highlander, 73, 74
*His Fifty Years of Exile; see Israel
    Potter*
History of Pittsfield, Massachusetts, 65
Hoadley, John C., 63, 64
Holmes, Oliver Wendell, 45, 52, 56
Holy Land, *M's* visit to the, 54–56, 129
Howard, Leon, 81
Humor, *M's* use of, 24–25
Hunilla ("The Encantadas"), 119

"I and My Chimney," 25, 53
Indomitable, 139
Irving, Washington, 40
Isabel (*Pierre*), 32, 106–108
Ishmael (*Moby-Dick*), 87, 91, 94, 95,
    96, 97, 98, 99, 106, 150, 151
Israel Potter, 44, 51, 61, 113–15, 151

Jackson (*Redburn*), 73
Jacksonian democracy, 80, 142
James, G. P. R., 45
James, Henry, 22
Jeroboam, 101
"Jimmy Rose," 53
John Marr and Other Sailors, 66, 124,
    127, 128, 145
Johnstone, Dr. Francis, 37, 75
Jonah, sermon on, 95, 100
Jones, John Paul, 114
Julia, 71
Jungfrau, 102

Kemble, Fanny, 45
Kostanza (*Mardi*), 79

Lady of the Lake, The, 132
Lansing, Abraham, 65
Lansing, Catherine, 65
Lansingburgh (N.Y.), *M's* life in, 17,
    32–34, 39

Lansingburgh Academy, 33
Lawrence, D. H., 24, 147
Lecturer, *M* as, 57
Library of American Literature, 146
Life in a Man-of-War, 74
"Lightning-Rod Man, The," 51, 115
Lincoln, Abraham, 58
Literary World, 41, 45, 46
Liverpool, *M's* voyage to, 33–34
Lizzie; *see* Melville, Elizabeth Shaw
Lombardo (*Mardi*), 79
Long Ghost, Dr. (*Omoo*), 37, 71, 73
Longman's (British publisher), 56
Lucy (Tartan) (*Pierre*), 106, 108
Lusiad, The, 39

Mackshane, Dr. 76
MacMechan, A. M., 146
Magazine writer, *M* as, 50–53
"Maldive Shark, The" (quoted), 124
"Malvern Hill," 127
Mapple, Father (*Moby-Dick*), 95, 100
"March to the Sea, The," 61, 126
Mardi, 19, 20, 21, 24, 26, 41, 42, 44, 46,
    47, 64, 72, 77, 78–83, 90, 106, 111,
    113, 123, 124, 134, 137, 138, 140,
    141, 142, 151, 153; publication of, 42
Margoth (*Clarel*), 76, 129, 132, 133, 143
Mariner's Sketches, A, 74
Marquesas Islands, 36–37, 69
Marryat, Captain, 73
Mather, Frank J., 147
Mathews, Cornelius, 45
Media, King (*Mardi*), 78, 79
Melvill, Allan (*M's* father), 29, 30, 31
Melvill, Maria Gansevoort (*M's* mother),
    29, 33, 54, 57, 63 [later *Melville*]
Melvill, Pierre Thomas (*M's* cousin), 32
Melvill, Priscilla (*M's* cousin), 32
Melvill, Robert (*M's* cousin), 44
Melvill, (Major) Thomas (*M's* grand-
    father), 29, 30
Melvill, (Major) Thomas (*M's* uncle),
    31, 32, 35, 65
Melville, Allan (*M's* brother), 30, 33,
    39, 41, 54, 58, 59, 60, 63, 64, 65
Melville, Augusta (*M's* sister), 30, 48,
    54, 64
Melville, Catherine (*M's* sister), 30
Melville, Elizabeth (*M's* daughter), 65

Melville, Elizabeth Shaw (*M's* wife), 39, 40, 41, 42, 45, 47, 48, 49, 52, 53, 54, 60, 61, 62, 64, 65, 66, 81; *M's* marriage to, 40–41
Melville, Frances (*M's* daughter), 52, 65
Melville, Gansevoort (*M's* sister), 30, 39, 41
Melville, Helen Maria (*M's* sister), 30, 39, 41
Melville, Malcolm (*M's* son), 48, 54, 63, 66
Melville, Thomas (*M's* brother), 30, 40, 57, 63, 64, 65
Melville Society, The, 148
Men of the Time, 146
Mercier, James, 74
Meteor, 57, 58
Meynell, Viola, 147
Milton, John, 90, 92, 130, 139, 140
"Misgivings, 1860," 127
Missionaries, *M's* criticism of, 69
Moby-Dick, 18, 19, 20, 21, 22, 23, 24, 25, 35, 44, 46, 47, 48, 49, 50, 66, 72, 74, 75, 78, 83–106, 111, 112, 122, 134, 135, 139, 141, 146, 147, 150–51, 152; publication of, 47; writing of, 44–45, 46–47
Mohi (*Mardi*), 78, 79
"Monody" (quoted), 61
Morewood, Robert, 45
Morewood, Mrs. R. J., 47
Mortmain (*Clarel*), 129
Mosses from an Old Manse, M's review of, 46, 93
Motteux, Peter, 82
Mumford, Howard, 128, 129
Murray, John (British publisher), 40, 68

Narrative of a Four Months' Residence among the Natives of a Valley of the Marquesas Islands; see Typee
Natural History of the Sperm Whale, 128
Navy, *M's* life in the, 38–39
Nehemiah (*Clarel*), 129, 132
Neversink, 21, 75, 76
New Bedford (Mass.), 35
New York City, *M's* birth in, 29; *M's* return to, 41, 60
New York Male High School, 30

North, Christopher; *see* Wilson, John

O'Brien, Fitz-James, 49
"O Captain, My Captain," 126
Ocean Tragedy, An, 145
Omoo, 21, 23, 24, 25, 37, 38, 40, 42, 44, 52, 66, 70–72, 75, 82, 83, 137, 146, 147, 151; publication of, 40

"Paradise of Bachelors and the Tartarus of Maids, The," 25, 51
Paradise Regained, 140
Passive resistance, 115–16, 152
Past and Present, 84
"Pasteboard masks" passage in *Moby-Dick* (quoted), 22, 85
Pease, Captain Valentine, Jr., 35, 36
Peleg, Captain Valentine, Jr., 35, 36
Peleg, Captain (*Moby-Dick*), 95, 96
Pequod, 35, 75, 86, 91, 95, 96, 97, 99, 101, 102, 103, 105, 106, 112
Peter Simple, 73
"Philip," 61
Philo Logos Society, 32
"Piazza, The," 25, 115
Piazza Tales, The, 49, 54, 115–119
Picture of Liverpool, 73
Pierce, Franklin, 49
Pierre, 19, 20, 24, 25, 26, 30, 31, 48, 49, 50, 72, 78, 106–11, 112, 113–34, 135, 137, 141, 149, 151; publication of, 48; writing of, 48
Pierre (Glendinning) (*Pierre*), 106–11, 150
Pip (*Moby-Dick*), 91, 104
Pittsfield (Mass.), *M* teaches school at, 32; *M's* life in, 45–59
Plinlimmon pamphlet, 110
Poe, Edgar Allen, 22, 117, 121
Poetry (of *M*), 20, 61, 64–65, 66, 67, 122–34, 152
Polk, James, 39
Polynesian Researches, 70, 128
"Poor Man's Pudding and Rich Man's Crumbs," 51
Putnam's Monthly Magazine, 49, 50, 51, 52, 53, 56, 62, 115, 119

Queequeg (*Moby-Dick*), 91, 94, 95, 96, 98, 103, 106

Rabelais, François, 24, 81-82
Rachel, 91, 102, 106
Realism in *M,* 111, 113, 149, 150
Redburn, 24, 34, 42, 44, 66, 72-74, 84, 136, 151; publication of, 42
Refugee, The, 61
Religion, *M's* attitude toward, 25-27, 54, 128-29, 130, 143-44, 149
"Returned Volunteer to His Rifle, The" (quoted), 127
Revivai, The Melville, 145-48
Richardson, Charles F., 87
Roderick Random, 74, 76
Rolfe *(Clarel),* 129
Rose-Bud, 102
Rousseau, Jean Jacques, 27
Rosenberry, Edward H., 24
Russell, W. Clark, 65, 66, 145, 146
Ruth *(Clarel),* 129
Rutland, Duke of, 43

Salt, H. S., 146
Samson Agonistes, 139
Samuel Enderby, 102, 103
Sandburg, Carl, 127
San Dominick, 117, 118
Sartor Resartus, 45, 83-86
Science, *M's,* view of, 25-27, 133, 143-44
Scoresby, William, Jr., 97
Scott, Sir Walter, 132
Sedgwick, Harry, 45
Sedgwick, William Ellery, 132
Serapis, 115
Serenia *(Mardi),* 80, 134
Shakespeare, William, 24, 44, 46, 106, 123, 126
Sharks, sermon on, 100-101
Shaw, Elizabeth; *see* Melville, Elizabeth Shaw
Shaw, (Judge) Lemuel *(M's* father-in-law), 39, 46, 49, 54, 56, 58
Shaw, Lemuel *(M's* brother-in-law), 65
Shaw, Samuel *(M's* brother-in-law), 62
Shelley, Percy Bysshe, 131
Shepherd, Daniel, 54
"Sheridan at Cedar Creek," 61, 126
"Shiloh: A Requiem" (quoted), 125
Small, Elisha, 66
Smith, J. E. A., 59, 65, 146

Smollett, Tobias, 74
Smythe, Henry, 62
Snow, Wilbert, 147
Social reform, *M's* attitude toward, 142-43
Somers affair, 39, 66-67, 139
Sources, *M's* use of, 22-24
South Seas, 17, 20, 69, 111, 146; *M's* adventures in the, 36-40; *M's* voyage to the, 35-36
"South Seas, The" (lecture), 57
Spencer, Philip, 39
Spenser, Edmund, 81
Stanly, Glen *(Pierre),* 107, 108
Stanwix, Fort, 29
Starbuck *(Moby-Dick),* 22, 85, 86, 89, 91, 96, 98
"Statues in Rome" (lecture), 57
Stedman, Arthur, 146
Stedman, Edmund Clarence, 146
Stevenson, Robert Louis, 146
Stewart, Charles S., 23, 70
St. Lawrence, 33-34, 42, 72
Stoddard, R. H., 146
"Story of Toby, The," 69
Stubb *(Moby-Dick),* 91, 96, 97, 99, 100
Style, *M's,* 20-24
Sumner, Charles, 58, 59
Symbols, *M's* use of, 20-22, 88-93

Tahiti, *M's* life in, 37-38, 70
Taipi tribe ("Typees"), 36
Taji *(Mardi),* 42, 78-80, 90, 91, 112
"Tartarus of Maids, The," 25
Tashtego *(Moby-Dick),* 97, 98, 112
Teufelsdröckh, Diogenes, 84, 86, 90
Theories of the Novel, *M's,* 121-22
Thomas, Henry B., 65
Thoreau, Henry David, 115, 142
Thorp, Willard, 19, 23, 67, 92, 128
Timoleon, 67, 127
Toby *(Typee): see* Greene, Richard Tobias
Tommo (Melville himself, in *Typee),* 37
Town-Ho, 99, 101
"Traveling" (lecture), 57
Troy, John B., 37, 71
Trumbull, Henry, 113
Twain, Mark, 114, 121
"Two Temples, The," 50

Two Years before the Mast, 72
Typee, 17, 20, 22, 23, 24, 25, 36, 40, 41, 42, 44, 46, 52, 67, 68-70, 71, 72, 82, 83, 111, 135, 137, 146, 147, 151; publication of, 40
Typees; *see* Taipi tribe

Ulver, Dolly (*Pierre*), 110
Undine, 81
Ungar (*Clarel*), 129
United States, 38, 39, 42, 74-75

Van Doren, Carl, 147
Vere, Captain (*Billy Budd*), 139, 140, 141-42
Vestiges of the Natural History of Creation, 128
Vincent, Howard P., 23
Vine (*Clarel*), 129
Virgil, 132
Visit to the South Seas, A, 23, 70

Vivenza (*Mardi*), 79

Ward, Artemus, 121
Warren, Robert Penn, 126
Weaver, Raymond M., 67, 146, 147, 148
Weeds and Wildings, 67
Wendell, Barrett, 18
White, Andrew Dickinson, 26
White-Jacket, 20, 21, 24, 38, 39, 42, 43, 44, 66, 72, 74-77, 84, 136, 146, 151; publication of, 42
Whitman, Walt, 26, 131, 146
Wiley and Putnam, 41, 68, 69
Wilson, John, 109
Wordsworth, William, 76, 84, 131

Yankee Doodle, 41
Yillah (*Mardi*), 79, 80, 135
Yoomy (*Mardi*), 78, 79